The Movie Script

TRUE History of
JESUS 2,000 Years Ago

Romeo Greco in Egypt

King Herod

Pontius Pilate

Yusef and Maryam

Caiaphas

Roman Soldiers

Based on the teachings of the Honorable Elijah Muhammad, Specific Bibical Verses and Historical Roman and Jewish Figures

Written by Rasheed L. Muhammad

MOVIE TREATMENT

JESUS was born 2,000 years after Moses. His mother's name was Mary and his father's name was Joseph. Mary (MARYAM) and Joseph (YUSEF) agreed to marry when very small children going to school. When Joseph and Mary grew to the age of fifteen and seventeen, Joseph went to Mary's father (IMRAN) and told him that he loved Mary and Mary loved him and that they wanted to get married. Joseph was a poor man, a commoner. He also was a carpenter by trade. So, Mary's father objected to her marriage to Joseph, a poor carpenter. Mary's father was a big wealthy man and a great architect.

One day IMRAN had to go away to another town, about twenty – five miles from his home and set up a temple, but before he left home, he instructed his daughter to take care of the livestock until he returns in three days. After IMRAN leaves on his journey, a great dust storm comes up, which made it very dark. Mary becomes frightened and sends a message to Joseph, telling him she needed help because her father had gone away. Joseph came over to Mary's house on a dark and cloudy day.

Months later, an old woman approached Joseph and told him that the child Mary was carrying was his child and the child would be a wonderful child, a prophet and teacher. She told him that the child was his. At first, Joseph denied it. But this woman knew because she was a prophetess, or what we call a medium. She told him the child's name was in the Holy Qur'an and that he should take care of him because the authorities will seek the child's life.

The last month of Mary's pregnancy drew near but the authorities did not know what time the child would be born. So the same medium that told Joseph of the child also went and told the authorities but no one knew which day the child would be born, although they knew the week.

The authorities had a committee to go around to take a census of all the pregnant women and when they would give birth. This committee checked everyone who was pregnant. When the week came that Jesus would be born, the authorities had given orders that all boy babies born in that week should be killed. Joseph took charge of Mary himself. He made one of the animal stalls on IMRAN'S property and filled it all around and inside with bales of hay and put a bed in the center. This was how JESUS was born in a manger. Months later, Joseph told Mary that he would have to send her and the child away to Cairo, Egypt. Mary took the child whom she named EASHUA (JESUS in Aramaic) on a fast mail camel.

In Egypt, JESUS was taught the law prophet Moses had revealed to the Jews. He was also taught how to read minds. After he finished school, he traveled to South Europe to the root of the Adamic Civilization. Herod, Caiaphas, the Jewish High Priest, Sejanus, Pontius Pilate, Tiberius, Caesar—the authorities in general chased him until he became discouraging to them so much so, a reward for his life was issued, $1,500 alive and $2,500 dead. They named him Christ (which means troublemaker) because every time they would get close to him, he would be gone.

JESUS returned to Jerusalem. Jewish socio-political, economic and religious leadership were totally compromised under Greek Hellenism. Their internecine religious wars and revolts set Roman against them. JESUS knew he would be killed but did not care after he realized how he was 2,000 years ahead of the time before Hellenism would be totally destroyed and the kingdom of peace established.

JESUS was age 36 when he allowed himself to be caught kill by a poor roman officer. He was not afraid. He was a brave man. He stood erect, stretched both his arms out across an old boarded up storefront in old Jerusalem. He died instantly upon impact when his heart was pierced.

FADE IN:

HERODS PALACE - DAY

ESTABLISHING

> NARRATOR (V.O.)
> The invasion of Alexander the Great, was a
> curse upon Jerusalem for centuries. The
> influence of Greek culture, its decadence,
> degeneration and language upset the ancient
> world of Jerusalem. So a child had to be born.
>
> Two-thousand year ago of the Hebrew year
> 3758, Jesus was born to Mary and Joseph in
> the town of Bethlehem. His purpose was to
> show forth a sign to come that would bring
> an end to the Adamic Civilization of the
> wicked. The Three wise men and the wicked
> knew the but no one knew the exact day of
> the child's birth.

EXT. PLAY GROUND - DAY

Fifteen children (6 - 9), all Afro-Asiatic ethnics, four Greeks playing on school playground. MARY (MARYAM in Aramaic) (6) black curly hair, dark brown skin and pretty tags JOSHEPH (YUSEF in Aramaic) (6), kinky black hair, smooth black skin and handsome tags her back and runs across a field of grass. In the f.g., two Greek children point at MARYAM chase YUSEF on a grassy hill. Both flapping their arms like two love birds.

> MARYAM
> I'm going to catch up to you.

> YUSEF
> You must learn to run faster.

MARYAM stubbles and falls. YUSEF sees her fall. He returns to help her stand. MARYAM brushes off some lose grass from her knees and elbows. See looks into YUSEF'S right eye slightly smiling and says, "Thank you YUSEF. In the b.g., the other children see them and begin pointing fingers and laughing. A Greek boy child, AEGEUS (6) blond hair blue eyes says to LEDA (6) red hair girl with blue eyes, says, "look at YUSEF, he likes MARYAM."

> AEGUES
> (sarcastically)
> You mean Joseph?

> LEDA
> Yes, YUSEF.

                              AEGUES
I think he likes that girl too

                              LEDA
Don't they look so cute?

                              AEGUES
I see them getting married one day.

                              LEDA
Ouuwe! He is going to get in some trouble.

                                                        CUT TO:

EXT. GRASSY FIELD – DAY

YUSEF and MARYAM stand facing toward the school playground.

                              YUSEF
                      (eyes cut left toward
                      maryam)
MARYAM, one day I am going to marry you.

                              MARYAM
                      (blushing, eyes cut right
                      toward yusef)
I will be waiting for you YUSEF.

                                                      FADE OUT:

INT. LIVING ROOM - EVENING

MARYAM sits on a couch reading a book in the living room of her father's opulent
home. Her father, IMRAN (35), brown skin, sturdy built, medium black beard, course
black hair and her mother ANAH (35), dark skin, silky black hair, medium built walk
into the living room. ANAH walks over and kisses MARYAM on the forehead. IMRAN
stands a distance away by the kitchen door.

                              IMRAN
                      (looks at his anah)
ANAH, I see our daughter reading a
book again.

                              MARYAM
Yes father. Mother knows I like to read.

IMRAN
What is the book about?

MARYAM
Our people's great past. It says our kings
established Jerusalem 1000's of years ago.

ANAH
And great it is. They built their palaces in
Jerusalem and good homes in Bethlehem.

MARYAM
Father did you know our ancestors have
been living in Jericho for over 9,000 years?

INRAM
(smiling)
Of course, sweet heart. Keep reading and
learning about yourself. You may even find
Araunah, my great, great, great grandfather
in your history book.

MARYAM
Was he wealthy like you?

IMRAN
Yes. He once owned the land where the
Jewish Temple sits today in Jerusalem.
(beat)
Of course, that was centuries ago before the
Jebusites were slaughtered and lost political
control of this city to the Jews. Afterward,
most of our people fled or migrated south-
west and to the farthest corners of the
earth.

MARYAM
(bright eyed)
Wow!

MARYAM sets the book down on a table. She looks at both her mother and father and
says, "I love you both so much. I will never forget your words."

FADE OUT:

EXT. DINING ROOM – EVENING

YUSEF sits in a chair at a modest size dining room table. Across from him sits his mother (HALEEMA) and step-father (HABIL). Everyone is enjoying dinner.

> HABIL
> How was school today YUSEF?

> YUSEF
> I learned several new math problems and
> how to help deliver babies.

> HALEEMA
> Oh YUSEF, I so proud of you son.

> HABIL
> YUSEF, one day I will teach you how to
> become a great carpenter if you keep up
> your math skills

> YUSEF
> That will be okay with me.

> HABIL
> And what is that son?

> YUSEF
> (eyes sparkling)
> I want to learn how to build houses.

HALEEMA gets you from the table. She walks over to YUSEF and kisses him on the forehead.

FADE OUT

INT. OPEN COURTYARD – ROOF – DAY

SUPERIMPOSE: 3 YEARS LATER

IMRAN, MARYAM, and her mother, ANAH, sitting in chairs on roof top open court yard enjoying the fresh air.

> IMRAN
> MARYAM, one of your school teachers has
> informed me that you and a boy named
> YUSEF are engaging in an awful lot of
> conversation?

                    MARYAM
Oh father, he is my best friend. We have
Been friends since we were six years old.

                    IMRAN
Best friend or not, I want you to be careful,
you here?

                    MARYAM
Alright.

                    ANAH
Besides, your father and I have big plans
for you one day. So keep you mind off of
boys for now.

MARYAM has a sad look on her face. She slowly gets up, hugs her mother and walks away.

INT. BEDROOM – EVENING

MARYAM lies on the bed reading a book. She closes the book and places it beneath her pillow. Then she lies on her right side, closes her eyes and falls to sleep.

                                        DISSOLVE:

INT. IMRAN'S FRONT YARD - NIGHT

FADE IN

SUPERIMPOSE: 6 YEARS LATER

YUSEF (17), handsome, curly hair, well build walks down well-lit cobble stone road. He approaches IMRANS opulent home. From a distance, he sees MARYAM (15), very tender eyes, petite, gorgeous, dressed in white long dress, long sleeve blouse, wavy black hair. IMRAN, full salt-n-pepper beard, white robe and red turban sit on a bench next to her.

                    IMRAN
Oh that looks like YUSEF approaching?

                    MARYAM
Yes, I called him.

                    IMRAN
How did you do that MARYAM?

                    MARYAM
Remember father, he and I have been close
friends since we were six years old.

YUSEF walks up to the steps of the house. He greets both MARYAM and IMRAN. He says, "Shlamah."(Peace in Aramaic tongue)

> IMRAN.
> Peace be to you also.

> MARYAM
> Shlamah, YUSEF.

> IMRAN
> How are you doing young man?

> YUSEF
> (nervous)
> I am fine sir.

IMRAN invites YUSEF to come inside the house. He enters the home and sees all of its opulence and trappings.

> CUT TO:

INT. OPEN COURT YARD – DOWN STAIRS – NIGHT

IMRAN and YUSEF sit around a table talking. MARYAM brings a kettle of tea, places it on the table and sits down next to her father. IMRAN pours both he and YUSEF a cup of tea.

> IMRAN
> What brings you here today? Where you
> called?
> > (looks a maryam)

> YUSEF
> I came over to see MARYAM. I thought, I
> thought-

> IMRAN
> (interrupts)
> -I hear she called for you?

MARYAM and IMRAN both laugh. YUSEF looks perplexed. He scratches his head.

> MARYAM
> I'm happy you came here tonight YUSEF-

> IMRAN
> -How can I help you YUSEF?

                        YUSEF
        Well sir, I came over to ask for your
        daughters hand in marriage. I love her
        and she loves me.

MARYAM and YUSEF look at one another with big smiles. IMRAN rears his head back,
he stands up and looks at both of them. He says, "MARYAM can you please excuse
YUSEF and I. We are going to talk outside on the porch."

INT. FRONT PORCH - NIGHT

BOTH IMRAN and YUSEF stand on front porch of house.

                        IMRAN
        Young man, I promised my late wife that
        our daughter will marry a wealthy man. I
        understand your work is carpentry and
        building small rough houses in South
        Europe?

                        YUSEF
        Yes sir.

Unexpectedly, MARYAM opens the front door. She stand beneath the door frame.

                        MARYAM
        Father what does that matter? Did not your
        Great, great grandfather start from humble
        beginnings?

                        IMRAN
        Now, now dear MARYAM, that's a whole
        other story.
                (beat)
        MARYAM, can please step into the house
        while I discuss this matter with YUSEF?

MARYAM looks at YUSEF. He steps off the porch. She closes the door.

                        IMRAN (cont')
                (speaking quietly)
        Now young man, I can't allow you to marry
        my daughter.

IMRAN stands on his porch looking down at YUSEF standing on the lawn. In the b.g.
MARYAM looks out the window.

                        IMRAN (cont')
        Young man, I don't want to see you
        around here anymore. Do you understand?

YUSEF turns around, head hanging low. He walks away into the darkness of night.

FADE OUT:

EXT. POOL OF SILOAM – NIGHT

The moon is full. YUSEF riding his donkey near the Pool of Siloam. He dismounts the donkey and walks to the Pool side. He looks down into the Chrystal clear water and sees the light of the moon gleaming off the water.

> YUSEF
> (thinking to himself)
> 'I may as well forget about ever marrying
> MARYAM. I am too poor. Her father is
> too rich. He owns much cattle and plenty
> of property around here.'

FADE TO BLACK

EXT. MARKET PLACE – DAY

FADE IN:

SUPERIMPOSE: SOUTH EUROPE CONSTRUCTION SITE

YUSEF walks around the grounds of construction site kicking a piece of wood. An OLD MAN, (45), grey-hair long stringy hair and beard; wrinkle olive tone skin walks up to him. In the b.g., several scruffy looking Caucasian males (30), pot bellies and Jebusites (25) light brown, curly hair, slim beards work on a small little rough home.

> OLD MAN
> What is your name?

> YUSEF
> I am YUSEF.

> OLD MAN
> Joseph, at some point you must marry
> someone else, have children and enjoy
> life.

> YUSEF
> (startled and surprised)
> I said my name is YUSEF!
> (beat)
> What you mean to say OLD MAN?

The OLD MAN slowly walks backward. He says, "Jospeh, your name will live thousands of years from now. But you must leave Southern Europe. Return to Palestine as soon as possible. Destiny awaits you.

YUSEF stares at the OLD MAN until he hears the voice of his construction FOREMAN bellow out, "YUSEF anytime you're ready to work, let me know." YUSEF turns around and walks toward his construction FOREMAN while at the same time looking backward at the OLD MAN.

                                                                    DISSOLVE

INT. LAVISH TENT – EVENING

SUPERIMPOSE: 7 YEARS LATER JERUSALEM

IMRAM host a gathering under a large tent near the pool of Siloam. The event is festive. In attendance are Jews, Greeks, Nubians and several Roman nobles. All guest are wearing their traditional cultural costumes.

IMRAN moves about the crowd introducing himself. In the b.g. three musicians, including one female (ages 16 - 19), tan skin, curly fine hair, fine features play a flute and string instruments.

                        NARRATOR (V.O.)
            IMRANS event appears to be successful. He
            has attracted the wealthiest people in and
            around Jerusalem; including several young
            men of wealth whom he desires to match
            with his daughter for matrimony.

EXT. POOL OF SILOAM - DAY

MARYAM stands next to the pool of SILOAM next to several other WOMEN. A male servant offers her a glass of wine. She declines, but the other WOMEN standing next to take the glasses. MARYAM notices, from a distance, her father standing with a handsome YOUNG MAN (Nubian) pointing in her direction.

                        MARYAM
                    (thinking to herself)
            My father is up something.

                        WOMEN 1
                    (looks at Maryam)
            Why is that man pointing in this direction?

                        MARYAM
            I don't know, but I have some idea.

                    WOMEN 2
Look, he's with that old man wearing the
gold color turban.

                    MARYAM
That old man is my father. He's sponsoring
this entire event.

                    WOMEN 3
What is your father's name?

                    MARYAM
IMRAN, he is an architect. Match maker
extraordinar.
          (quietly chuckles)

                    WOMEN 4
He looks very fit for this age. I wish
him well sister MARYAM.

All the women laugh and giggle.

INT. LAVISH TENT - EVENING

IMRAN makes a toast with the handsome YOUNG NUBIAN male. The two glasses of tea
cling to together. In the f.g., MARYAM sits on a polished granite stone bench with two
other women.

                    IMRAN
          (grinning from ear to ear)
What did you say your name was again?

                    YOUNG NUBIAN
KHAPERRE, sir.

                    IMRAN
KHAPERRE, it was a pleasure to meet you.
I will be setting up a date when you and
my daughter should meet.

                    KHAPERRE
Well sir, from a distance, she appears to
be a very lovely women. I sincerely hope
to meet you both soon in Cairo, Egypt

                    IMRAN
We will see you soon KHAPERRE.
          (beat)
Tell your father I look forward to working
on his big project near the Nile River.

KHAPERRE
I certainly will sir.

EXT. POOL OF SILOAM – SUNSET

INRAM and MARYAM sit on the granite stone bench alone near the Pool of Siloam. In the f.g., male servants clean up and break down the tent. The sound of water splashes against the pools edge. Both MARYAM and her father watch the sunset.

IMRAN
How did you enjoy our event MARYAM?

MARYAM
It was a great way to make the citizens
of Jerusalem feel special.

IMRAN
It also means more business for me and
the future of the family.

MARYAM
(curiously)
Father, who was that young man you were
talking with earlier today?

IMRAN
(elated)
Oh! He is a wealthy young noble of Cairo,
Egypt. His name is KHAPERRE. I plan to
take you with me to Cairo one day soon
to meet him and his family.

MARYAM
(hesitantly)
Father, what are you proposing to me?

IMRAN
Well dear, I think just maybe he will make
an excellent husband.

MARYAM
(defiantly)
How could you?

IMRAN
Will you at least think about it?

MARYAM
(hesitantly)
Yes father, for you I will think about it.

EXT. HOME OF YUSEF – DAY

FADE IN:

SUPERIMPOSE: NAZERETH

YUSEF (27), neatly trimmed mustache sits on a rug beneath a tree behind his small house on a plot of land. In the b.g., his wife, SAMAYYAH slender built, pretty, curly long hair, brown skin watches their SIX CHILDREN (four boys and two girls ages 2 - 12) pick vegetables from a garden. SAMAYYAH walks up to YUSEF. She gives him a gentle lip kiss.

                    YUSEF
          SAMAYYAH it's such a lovely evening
          today.
                    (takes deep breath)
          Can you feel the power of the earth?

                    SAMAYYAH
          Yes it is sweet heart. We are thankful for
          what we have. Our children will do well
          for themselves.

The youngest daughter runs up to YUSEF, she says with excitement, "daddy, daddy". She hands YUSEF a tomato. As he kisses her on the forehead.

                    YUSEF
                    (looks at baby girl)
          Honey go back to the garden with your
          other brothers and sisters and eat as many
          tomatoes as your heart desires.

SAMAYYAH gently crabs her daughter's hand and says, "let your father rest" as they both walk toward the garden.

                                             CUT TO:

INT. INRAMS RICH HOME – DAY

MARYAM sits alone in a large living room surrounded by opulence, paintings, plants, embroidered chairs, couches and redwood tables. She is reading a book. Her father walks into the living room smiling, humming a happy song.

                    IMRAN
          MARYAM, have you thought going to
          Cairo with me?

MARYAM stands to her feet. She walks over to the window and says softly, "no father, I have not" thought about it."

IMRAN
Then what's on your mind, MARYAM.

MARYAM
(turns around)
If I cannot marry YUSEF, then I will not
marry anyone. Father please respect my
decision.

MARYAM slowly walks away from the window, up the wooden stairway into her
bedroom.

INRAM walks over to the couch. He lies down and begins rubbing his head. He looks up
at the ceiling. It appears to be spinning around and around.

NARRATOR (V.O.)
INRAM is worried. He knows YUSEF is a
poor commoner, a second rate carpenter
working mostly on small rough homes in
South Europe. The more he thought about
his daughter never marrying, the more he
thought about her becoming an old maid.

In the holy land, all men desire their
daughters marry good men. So INRAM was
becoming sick believing that he would
never become a grandfather.

FADE TO BLACK

EXT. INRAMS HOME – GROUNDS – MORNING

MARYAM walks around the grounds of her father's estate. She hears to sound of birds
tweeting, she admirers flower beds, grazing sheep and cattle down the sloppy hill. She
places a blanket on a patch of grass beneath a fig tree and sits down. From a distance,
she sees IMRAN approaching her riding on his horse.

IMRAN
(dismounts horse)
MARAYAM, I must speak with you now.

MARYAM
Ou! Father, what is it? Are you alright?

IMRAN
(sense of urgency)
Yes, please walk with around the estate.

They both walk down the hillside slope toward the sheep and cattle where the animal
stalls are constructed.

NARRATOR (V.O)
INRAM was going to another town about
twenty-five miles from his home to set
up a Temple. He gave MARYAM some
very careful instructions how maintain
the estate while he was gone.

IMRAN
Now daughter, I have to go away. I'll be
gone for about three days. You must
take care of everything until I return.
You must feed and water livestock.

MARYAM
(energetic)
I think I can handle that.

INT. INSIDE ANIMAL STALL – DAY

IMRAN and MARYAM standing inside an animal stall.

IMRAN
Now MARYAN, I want you to wear my
old clothes and put on some false
whiskers so people, when they see
you going down to feed the stock, they
think you are me and no one will say
anything to you.

MARYAM lifts up the old clothes and plays around with the whiskers by placing it on
her face.

FADE TO BLACK

EXT. DARK CLOUDY SKY – MORNING

MARYAM walks outside. She looks up into the sky. A dust storm is approaching. The
morning sky is becoming dark. She becomes frightened, runs back into the house and
scrambles into her bedroom. While sitting on the edge of her bed, she closes her eyes.

NARRATOR (V.O)
MARYAM sends a message to YUSEF by
concentrating on him. She tells YUSEF
that her father has gone away for three
days and she was left to feed and water
livestock.

MARYAM (O.S.)
I am alone and a little afraid.

NARRATOR (V.O.)
MARYAM ask YUSEF to come over to help
her take care to everything and to be
company with her.

ENT. BEDROOM OF YUSEF - MORNING

YUSEF awakens from his bed sweating. He sits up in bed and wiggles his right ear with his index-finger. He thinks to himself, 'I know I did not hear MARYAMS voice asking for help.' He gets up out of the bed and begins dressing himself.

YUSEF walks into the kitchen where his wife and children eat flat bread and fruit.

SAMAYYAH (P.O.V)
Honey you look like you just saw a ghost.

All six children laugh and giggle pointing at YUSEF.

YUSEF
(bewildered)
I'm sorry, honey but I must ride over to
Bethlehem to take care of some business.

SAMAYYAH
In this dust storm?

YUSEF
I think I can manage it.

SAMAYYAH
That's fine.
(beat)

YUSEF grabs a piece of flat bread off the table. He walks out the door.

SAMAYYAH
Be careful YUSEF!

FADE OUT

EXT. OLD ROAD TO BETHLEHEM – MORNING DUST CLOUDS

YUSEF wearing a grey over his head riding a donkey on an old dirt road. The dust storm is lightly blowing. He sees sign off to the side of the road reading 10 miles to BETHLEHEM.

EXT. IMRANS ESTATE – NOON

YUSEF at the front door. MARYAM peeps out the window. She opens the door and invites him inside. He walks into the house. MARAYAM quickly slams the door shut to prevent sand from entering the home.

                    YUSEF
          I heard your message so I came as
          quickly as possible.

MARYAM hugs YUSEF and says, "thank you for coming YUSEF." He looks around.

                    YUSEF
          Hurry MARYAM, give me the old man's
          costume so when anyone sees us, they
          will think I am the old man with you.

                    MARYAM
          Right, the livestock must be feed now.

YUSEF and MARYAM dress in separate rooms. Then they walk outside down the hillside slope to feed the livestock.

EXT. ANIMAL STALL – NOON

YUSEF and MARYAM walk into each stall and feed the sheep. The last stall they enter was empty. The wind is howling. YUSEF organizes bales of hay while MARYAM rest on a wooden bench petting a little lamb.

                                        FADE TO BLACK:

INT. DINNING ROOM – EVENING

YUSEF looks fresh and clean sitting at the dining room table finishing a meal. MARYAM enters the dining room. She seems to glow standing off to the side of the table.

                    YUSEF
          The meal was great.

                    MARAYAM
               (blushing)
          Thank you.

                    YUSEF
          We can keep meeting like this.

MARAYAM walks into the kitchen. She grabs a carrot and starts to slowly slice it. With her head down, she smiles.

                                        FADE OUT:

EXT. OLD ROAD – LATE EVENING

FADE IN:

YUSEF gazes up at the stars riding his donkey. Then he looks at a sign off to the side of the road reading 9 miles to Nazereth.

INT. PORCH – NIGHT

YUSEF dismounts his donkey. He walks up two steps onto the porch of his house. He enters the front door, walks to the living room couch. He lays down and immediately falls asleep.

FADE OUT:

EXT. TOWN MARKET PLACE - MORNING

The town market place is busy with merchants, buyers and sellers of every spice, vegetable, fruit, fish, lamb and beef. SAMAYYAH and the six CHILDREN sale vegetables from a table at the market place. On their table are tomatoes, garlic and figs.

EXT. IMRANS ESTATE – DAY

YUSEF and MARYAM stand around the grazing sheep. In the f.g., the cattle eat grass. A little lamb walks over and stands in between MARYAM and YUSEF. The lamb begins to baaa!!! MARYAM and YUSEF laugh. Then they both walk into a stall full of bales of hay. MARYAM begins to remove the fake beard. Outside, the cows begin to moou!!!

FADE TO BLACK:

EXT. PORCH – LATE EVENING

YUSEF is walking down the steps of IMRANS front porch. MARYAM watches him inside the house looking through the window. He stops, turns around and bows his head.

> MARYAM
> (lips moving)
> Shlamah

> YUSEF
> (lips moving)
> Shlamah

YUSEF smiles, turns around and begins walking into the night.

EXT. OLD ROAD – NIGHT

YUSEF is pulling his donkey by the harness. Other travelers on the road point at YUSEF and his stubborn donkey. YUSEF makes attempts to cover his face as he moves along.

ENT. PALACE OF HEROD – DAY

FADE IN:

SUPERIMPOSE: RIEGN OF AUGUSTUS CAESUR

Three WISE MEN (60), black, brown and red skin, beards, wearing white robes and white turbans stand outside the grand office door of HEROD, military Governorate of Rome (50), half black and half white Jew, pot belly, bald head, bushy beard and mean spirited. Two armed Roman guards stand watch at the entrance of the grand doors. Suddenly, a loud voice can be heard through the door, "Guards, let them enter."

The WISE MEN enter a plush Hellenistic Greek styled office. HEROD makes a gesture for them to sit down on huge cushy couch. HEROD has gold rings on eight fingers.

HEROD
Welcome to my humble abode. I am
HEROD, the military Governor of
Jerusalem. I serve Rome in this
providence.
(beat)
And yes, you may refer to me as HEROD.

WISE MAN 1
Thank you HEROD for allowing us to meet
with you.

HEROD
You see that statue over my shoulder?

WISE MAN 1
Yes…

HEROD
He was the last Hasmonean prince,
Mattathias Antigonus before Rome
appointed me "King of the Jews."
(big haughty laugh)
He was the first and the last prince
To call me a half Jew.
(beat)
Now what is it that you desire to share
with me?

WISE MAN 1
Yes, yes; of course.

WISE MAN 2
Since time is short. We will get right to
the point.

WISE MAN 1
HEROD a special women is about the
give birth to a special child in Jerusalem.
The book says he is destined to rule.

WISE MAN 3
The prophecy says this child will be
God in the flesh whose mission is to
establish a new kingdom of peace that
shall last forever and all others rulers
and kings shall throw their crowns at his
feet.

HEROD
(pulls his beard)
The last I checked, the Imperial cult of
Rome has declared Caesar Augustus as
the son of god, Romans divine ruler.

HEROD slowly stands to his feet holding his golden goblet. He looks at all three WISE
MEN with jaundice eyes.

HEROD (cont')
I appreciate your wise council, but we
also have a committee of religious
scholars reviewing the old Hebrew books
of prophecy from some channels among
the Hebrews living in Qumran and the
Dead Sea region.

The three WISE MEN notice HEROD was very nervous.

WISE MAN 2
I might add HEROD, the prophecy further
says the child will have an army of 10,000
soldiers when he becomes of age. Although
we cannot give you the exact day of this
birth, we do know the week.

HEROD
Our committee will take your words into
consideration and I will prepare to any
measure to protect my province.
(beat)
No if you will excuse me, I must leave.

HEROD immediately walks out of his office mumbling beneath his breath, "I am he
king of the Jews. I must go to Rome to warn Caesar."

The three WISE MEN look at one another with discernment and grin.

WISE MAN 3
Brothers, let us leave this decadent palace.
HEROD is a wickedly evil man. He has
been corrupted under Hellenists for
Rome's power and prestige. Neither he nor
Rome shall calculate the exact day of the
child's birth.

All three WISE MEN jump to their feet. They swiftly exit HEROD'S office, walk down the corridor. Once they get outside, all three men look up at the northern sky at its brightest star.

FADE TO BLACK

EXT. MARKET PLACE – DAY

FADE IN:

SUPERIMPOSE: CITY OF JERICHO

The market place is bustling with merchants. Hundreds of Jebusites, black men, women and children shop for goods. YUSEF walks about smiling and speaking with everyone. A young dark skin black boy, long wavy hair stands on the corner holding a basket of dried fish. YUSEF approaches him and purchase several pieces of dried fish. Out of nowhere, an OLD WOMEN (75), green head rap, colorful flowing beige long dress, very light skin, hazel eyes slightly bumps into YUSEF.

OLD WOMEN
(speaking in lowered voice)
Oh, excuse me YUSEF.

YUSEF
Pardon me. How do you know my name?

OLD WOMEN
I know more than you think.

YUSEF
Well what do you want, old women.

OLD WOMEN
Come, let us walk and talk away from the
crowd.

YUSEF and the OLD WOMEN slowly walk down the street away from the crowd. He begins to shake his head left to right several times.

NARRATOR (V.O.)
The OLD WOMEN tells YUSEF that he is
the father of the child and the girl, MARYAM,

is carrying his baby. At first YUSEF tried to
deny it. The OLD WOMEN goes on to tell
him that the child will be a wonderful child,
a prophet and a teacher. YUSEF denies her
claim again. So the OLD WOMEN tells YUSEF
that she is a prophetess or medium and his
child's name is found in the Holy Quran.

The OLD WOMEN looks up directly into the eyes of YUSEF. She places both her hands
on the side of his arms around the elbows.

> OLD WOMEN
> YUSEF, you will do well to take care of the
> child because the authorities will seek his
> life.

YUSEF looks straight into the greens eyes of the OLD WOMEN. He thinks to himself, "I
must warn MARYAM as soon as possible."

> YUSEF
> Where are you from?

> OLD WOMEN
> (grins)
> My name is Anna. I am from the Dead Sea
> region.

                                                        CUT TO:

EXT. IMRAN ESTATE GROUNDS – NOON

MARYAM is sitting on large pillows in a patch of grass beneath a fig tree, reading a book.
She sees her father riding his horse up the cobble stone path leading up to the house.
He dismounts his horse and begins walking towards MARYAM.

EXT. FIG TREE - NOON

IMRAN walks under the tree, yawns and stretches his arms out.

> MARYAM
> Father are you feeling well?

MARYAM stands up and hugs her father.

> IMRAN
> I'm just a little tired.

> MARYAM
> Well I miss you. You've been gone three
> days.

                         IMRAN
              I miss you too. How is it going?

                         MARYAM
                   (coy and hesitant)
              After the dust storm past, all went well.

MARYAM slowly takes three steps backward away from her IMRAN.

                         IMRAN
                   (tired expression)
              Do you mind if I sit under the fig tree
              to rest my weary bones?

                         MARYAM
              But of course, be my guest.

IMRAN lays down on a lush patch of grass. He falls asleep. MARYAM walks back to the house.

                                                  FADE OUT:

INT. KITCHEN – IMRANS HOME -NIGHT

FADE IN

SUPERIMPOSE: THREE MONTHS LATER

MARYAM looks out a window in the living room. The faint sound of crickets can be heard outside. IMRAN is sitting in his comfort chair eating dates and sipping on hot tea. He looks over at MARYAM.

                         IMRAN
              Hmmmmm!

MARYAM turns around and says, "What is the matter father?"

                         IMRAN
              I notice you are growing a little larger.
              What's a matter with you fattening so
              fast? Are you eating more than you
              should?

                         MARYAM
                   (startled)
              No father, I am not eating more than I
              should.

MARYAM begins to walk to the front door. IMRAN calls her back with a low tone, "MARYAM, where are you going." She stops.

> MARYAM
> (anxious)
> Yes father.

> IMRAN
> (concerned)
> MARYAM, there is something the matter
> with you. Look how large you are. What
> are you doing?

> MARYAM (P.O.V.)
> (speaks forthright)
> Okay father. I must confess. I must tell
> you the truth.

IMRAN tilts his head to the side. He looks up and down at MARYAM with a suspicious eye.

> MARYAM (cont')
> Do you remember when you went off to
> setup a temple and were gone for three
> days some time ago and left me to attend
> the livestock?
>
> Well, I was afraid because of a dust storm
> so sent for YUSEF to come over to help me.
> (beat)
> Well, he came and did help me feed the
> stock.

> IMRAN
> (deep voice, pulling his beard)
> Yes, and he fed them too!

> MARYAM
> (nervous)
> Do you remember YUSEF and me were
> trying to get you to let us marry when
> we were young and you would not allow
> us? Now this is what happened and I will
> send for YUSEF and let him tell you
> himself.

INRAM slowly turns around and drags himself upstairs to his room. He lies down in bed. He begins pulling whiskers from his chin until he falls asleep. MARYAM walks up the stairs to the roof top. She sees the sun setting. When she looks north, she sees YUSEF from a distance running toward the house.

EXT. ROOF TOP – EVENING

MARYAM and YUSEF stand on the roof top. A slight wind blows through MARYAM'S curly black hair dangling below her shoulders.

                    YUSEF
               (breathing heavy)
          I came as fast I could MARYAM to tell
          you what an old women told me.

                    MARYAM
          What are talking about YUSEF? What old
          women? And what did she say?

                    YUSEF
               (taking fast)
          She said you our pregnant with my child.
          She said she was a prophetess or what
          some call a medium. She said the
          authorities will seek the life of our child.

YUSEF places his right hand gently on MARYAM'S large stomach. She closes her eyes, a tear drops from her left eye.

                    MARYAM
          YUSEF, this is good news. You must tell
          my father right away. I tried to tell him
          what happened but he fell ill.

                    YUSEF
          Where is he now?

                    MARYAM
          In his bedroom.

MONTAGE – VARIOUS

- YUSEF walking down stairway from the roof top

- He stands at bedroom doorway entrance and sees IMRAN lying in bed sleeping

- IMRAN sits up in bed, YUSEF notices some of IMRANS hair is missing on his chin

 - YUSEF is sitting at end of bed talking to IMRAN

                    NARRATOR (V.O)
          YUSEF slowly walks down the hallway.
          He stands at the bedroom doorway and
          sees IMRAN lying in bed sick. YUSEF

begins to tell MARYAMS father about
everything. He reminds IMRAM how both
he and MARYAM loved each other, even
when we were going to school and promised
to marry at age six.

END MONTAGE

YUSEF
Remember when I came to you to asked for
your daughters hand but you forbade us to
marry?
(beat)
Now this is what happened.

FLASH BACK TO:

EXT. JERICHO MARKET PLACE - DAY

OLD WOMEN
YUSEF you are the father of the child and
the girl, MARYAM, is carrying his baby.

YUSEF
I don't have any children by MARYAM.

OLD WOMEN
Don't worry, the child will be a wonderful
child, a prophet and a teacher.

YUSEF
But I do not have a child by MARYAM.

OLD WOMEN
YUSEF, I am a prophetess or medium. My
name is Anna and the child's name is
found in the Holy Quran. You will do well
to take care of him because the
authorities will seek his life.

BACK TO PRESENT.

INT. IMRAN'S BEDROOM - NIGHT

IMRAN sits up against headboard of his bed. His health seems to return upon hearing
YUSEF'S speak.

                    YUSEF
                (looking at Imran)
So you can kill me for what I have secretly
done with MARYAM. I am the father of the
child that MARYAM is carrying but
remember the child is going to be a great
man, a prophet and teacher. His name can
be found in the history of the Holy Qur'an.

YUSEF looks toward the ground.

                    IMRAN
Continue young man.

                    YUSEF
Now remember, you must not tell anyone
about this because of the authorities. If
they knew this, they would kill the child.
So keep your mouth shut about this. Now
you can kill me if you want. I have told
you the truth.

                                        CUT TO:

SERIES OF SHOTS

(A) Old Prophetess women sitting in HEROD'S office surrounded by his staff. The table
    is full of food and drink. She partakes of none of it.

(B) Roman Government census workers search door to door questioning all pregnant
    women at their door steps

(C) ROMAN OFFICERS walk twelve little black boys down the streets of Bethlehem

                    NARRATOR (V.O)
The last week of MARYAM'S pregnancy
draws nigh. The old prophetess women
warns HEROD about the birth of the child,
but she does not know the exact day, only
the week of his birth. So the authorities
had a committee to go around from home
to home taking a census of all women who
were pregnant. When the week came that
Jesus would be born, the authorities had
given orders that all boy babies born in
that week should be killed.

END SERIES OF SHOTS

FLASH BACK TO:

EXT. DEPOT STORE – LATE EVENING

SUPRIMPOSE – 2 WEEKS EARLIER

IMRAN walks down a street. Several people walk by him and speak. Two Germanized ROMAN OFFICERS walk by. They stare him down. IMRAN enters a depot store. STORE CLERK, (19), tall skinny, brown skin, curl afro, mild mannered male greets IMRAN.

> STORE CLERK
> Shlamah brother IMRAN.

> IMRAN
> Peace my brother. What is going in the
> streets of Bethlehem this evening?

> STORE CLERK
> Last week, ROMAN OFFICERS made house
> to house searches. They were taking a
> census of all our pregnant women. The
> people are very upset after several boys
> as young as two years old were taken
> away.

> YUSEF
> Were are they?

> STORE CLERK
> Yes, they were all returned.

IMRAN walks over to the store window. He observes the expressions on the faces of the people outside and thinks to himself, "its happening as the old prophetess told YUSEF." IMRAN turns around toward the STORE CLERK.

> IMRAN
> Young man, can you deliver 24 bales of
> hay to my home tonight?
> > (beat)
> I also need seven more stables built in the
> morning. As you know I have plenty of
> livestock. I will pay extra, in gold coins to
> get all work done as fast as possible.

> STORE CLERK
> Right away my brother. I will have a work
> crew over to your estate early morn.

BACK TO PRESENT.

INT. INSIDE ANIMAL STALL – NIGHT

FADE IN:

SUPERIMPOSE: MONTH OF TISHRI
              HEBREW RELIGIOUS YEAR 3758

YUSEF places extra bales of hay and food around the walls inside the stall. He places piles of fluffy pillows and blankets on a wooden frame bed in the center of the stall. IMRAN helps walk a very pregnant MARYAM into the stall and he leaves. She lies down on the bed.

                    MARAYAM
              (smiles looking at yusef)
          I see you made me a nice cozy bed in this
          manger?

                    YUSEF
          Yes. From the outside, this it will look
          like a stall for the sheep. The extra hay
          will conceal and absorb sound to protect
          you and the baby from the authorities.

MONTAGE – VARIOUS

SLOW MOTION:

-YUSEF observes MARYAM in her birth pangs.

-Sheep baa's and meh's are unusually loud

-MARYAM is screaming at YUSEF

-YUSEF holds the baby and clips the umbilical cord

-The BABY is drinking MARYAM breast milk wrapped in a white blanket

                    NARRATOR (V.O.)
          YUSEF took charge of MARYAM himself. All
          men over in Asia are taught how to take care
          of their wives and perform this duty of child
          birth in cases when they don't care for a wet
          nurse.

          Alas, the black child is secretly born in as it was
          written, in a manger.

END OF MONTAGE

EXT. FIELD – LATE EVENING

From on a hill top, a dozen ROMAN OFFICERS nail several bearded orthodox Jews to crosses. Red blood dribbles down the wooden planks. The Roman commanding officer smirks and says, "on the orders of HEROD, this is the last of the rebels." He turns his head to the left. In the b.g., is HEROD'S palace surrounded by Roman guards holding flames of fire on long poles.

CUT TO:

EXT. IMRANS ESTATE GROUNDS – NOON

FADE IN:

Five government CENSUS TAKERS, two AFRICANIZED ROMAN OFFICERS, and three GERMANIZED OFFICERS, in uniform stand on IMRAN'S porch. One of them bangs on the front door. IMRAN opens the door wearing a thick house robe. In the b.g., he sees three Roman chariots parked on his grass.

> IMRAN
> (calmly looking)
> Yes, may I help you?

> CENSUS TAKER 1
> (threatening)
> Where is the women who gave birth this
> week?

> CENSUS TAKER 2
> (stern)
> Doesn't she live here?

> IMRAN
> What women?

> CENSUS TAKER 1
> The one that was with child!

> IMRAN
> (steps forward onto
> his porch)
> Oh, I know what you are talking about.
> The woman that was here some time ago.
> She was only visiting here, and has return
> to her home in Egypt.

Censure TAKER 2 looks around IMRAN'S left shoulder peering into his living room.

                    CENSUS TAKER 4
                  (lifts left eyebrow)
              Oh she was just visiting?

                        IMRAN
                      (humble)
                Yes, that is all.

                  AFRICANIZED OFFICER 1
              We might return, so be careful what you say old
              man.

INT. BACK SEAT OF CHARIOT - NOON

AFRICANIZED ROMANS driving chariot. CENSUS TAKER 2 sitting across from CENSUS TAKER 1 in the back seat of chariot. He says, "damn, we miscalculated the exact day and location where the child should be born."

                    CENSUS TAKER 2
              I don't trust that Jebusite.

                                                        DISSOLVE:

EXT. ESTATE OF IMRAN - MORNING

SUPERIMPOSE: FOUR MONTHS LATER

YUSEF climbs down a ladder on IMRANS home. He walks over to the back door and grabs a bag of food and water. In the f.g., IMRAN is attending to some cattle on the estate grounds.

INT. INSIDE MANGER - MORNING

YUSEF overlooking MARYAM and the child, black and beautifully glowing skin, hair like lamb's wool. Both are sleeping. He sets the food and water by the side of the bed and leaves.

                                                        DISSOLVE:

EXT. COBBLE STONE PATHWAY - DAY

YUSEF walks his donkey up the cobble stone pathway alongside IMRAN'S home. IMRAN meets YUSEF at the gate entrance.

                      NARRATOR (V.O.)
                YUSEF arrived daily with water and food
                to see MARYAM and the baby. He fooled
                his wife by telling her that he had a job
                building a house.

INT. IMRANS INNER COURTYARD - DAY

IMRAN and YUSEF stand face to face beneath a Palm leaves planted in the courtyard.

IMRAN
Son, it's not safe here anymore for
MARYAM and the baby.

YUSEF
I know. I am waiting for another dust
storm. That way I can send MARYAM
and EASHOA to Cairo with his own
people of Nubia.

IMRAN
I'm glad you and my daughter finally
decided on a name for the baby?

YUSEF
Yes, yes. EASHOA in Aramaic or E-SHO
meaning, giver of life.
(beat)
MARYAM and I refuse to give him a name
after the Greeks.

IMRAN
As it should be. Our mother tongue is
Aramaic, not common Greek.
(laughs)
If we are not careful, one day, they will call
him Jesus, after their mother tongue.
(beat)
YUSEF, I think the child has a good name
and meaning...giver of life. I also think it's
a good idea to send them to Cairo among
his own people. I have a property down their
too.

DISSOLVE:

INT. MANGER - MORNING

SERIES OF SHOTS

(1) YUSEF brings more food and water for MARYAM and JESUS

(2) YUSEF watches MARYAM breast feed the baby. His chocolate brown skin and white pearly eyes sparkle

(3) MARYAM hands the baby to YUSEF as he gently rocks JESUS to sleep

(4) YUSEF riding Donkey on old road. He see a sign off the side of the road reading 19 miles to NAZERETH

(5) YUSEF walks up to his home, donkey in tow. His wife and six children are relaxing in the front yard. Everyone looks happy.

(6) YUSEF places several silver and gold coins into the palm of his wife.

(6) MARYAM sits in the manger near a cozy fire reading a book to the baby. He smiles and grabs the book

END SERIES OF SHOTS

EXT. ATOP A HILLSIDE – NOON

FADE IN:

YUSEF and SAMAYYAH stand on hillside looking down at HEROD'S PALACE. Inside they see Jebusites and others engaging in a party of orgies, drunkenness and sacrificing of a pig at an altar. SAMAYYAH says to herself, "the spreading of Greek culture has influenced our ancient world with decadence and indecency. They have stolen our wealth, ruined our ties, local loyalties and true ambitions. I pray JESUS can bring about a change to our world."

FADE OUT:

EXT. MANGER - EVENING

FADE IN:

YUSEF walks into manger. MARYAM says, Shlamah and gently hands him the baby. YUSEF kisses he baby on the forehead. He smiles and kicks his feet. YUSEF hands the baby back over the MARYAM.

> YUSEF
> MARYAM, I must send you and the
> JESUS to Cairo, Egypt to live among
> his own people. It is too dangerous
> here in Palestine. You leave upon the
> next dust storm.

FADE TO BLACK:

EXT. CAMEL STATION – DUST STORM - DAY

The day has become darkened with the dust storm overhead. MARYAM and JESUS dismount a donkey at the camel station. JESUS is sound asleep snuggly rapped in a green sheet tied to the front of MARYAMS upper body. In the f.g. a camel attendant is bringing one hump back camel over to MARYAM and YUSEF. The camel bends down on her front knees. The attendant helps MARYAM mount the camel. YUSEF pays the attendant. He gives MARYAM some food and money. Then whispers into the ear of the camel.

> NARRATOR (V.O.)
> YUSEF whispers into the mail camel's
> ear, 'take them to Cairo.' Then away
> they went for the camel station to
> Cairo where in Asia camel stations are
> the best means of transportation. The
> camel is very sensitive and a fast
> runner. The mail camels go from forty
> to fifty miles per hour and it was one of
> the mail camels YUSEF hired that knew
> the route to Egypt well. So MARYAM and
> JESUS were on their way to Egypt.

SERIES OF SHOTS

(1) A camel races across the desert by night with MARYAM and JESUS riding on its hump back

(2) From a distance, a full moon can be seen above the sand dunes

(3) In the valley below, three pyramids shine brightly from the moons light

END SERIES OF SHOTS

EXT. DIRT ROAD - NIGHT

YUSEF riding his donkey on a dirt road leading up to his house. Straight ahead, he sees a light flickering behind a window curtain of his home. A faint sound of two cats fighting from some unknown alleyway.

FADE TO BLACK:

EXT. CAMEL STATION – MORNING

FADE IN:

SUPERIMPOSE: EGYPT, CAIRO

MARYAM, wearing a purple garment to her ankles, hair and face fully covered with a purple scarf, except for her eyes arrives at the camel station in Cairo. She sees dozens of other people leaving and arriving at the station. The double hump back camel lowers his knees onto ground. She dismounts with the help of a camel ATTENDANT (18), brown skin male wearing brown robe, short curly hair.

                    ATTENDANT
Welcome to Cairo.

                    MARYAM
Thank you, Can up take us to the town of
Giza?

                    ATTENDANT
Yes my sister. I can take you and your child.

EXT. BOAT ON NILE RIVER – MORNING

MARYAM sits in back seat of small reed boat holding JESUS in her lap. She removes her scarf from over her face. A slight breeze blows through her hair. The baby laughs and giggles. The ATTENDANT sits in the rear of the boat with paddles guiding the reed boat down the river.

EXT. BOAT DEPOT – DAY

MARYAM and JESUS exit the boat. They are surrounded by dozens of his MALE and FEMALE RELATIVES (ages 8 to 80). Everyone is greeting MARYAM with smiles and adoring the baby.

                    MALE RELATIVE 1
We hope your journey was not too rough for
you and the child.

                    MARYAM
                 (holding the baby)
The mail camel was very experienced with the
route to Cairo.

                    FEMALE RELATIVE 2
You and the baby must be exhausted. Let's go
now to the apartment.

                    MARYAM
It's walking distance?

                    MALE RELATIVE 2
Yes, it's not far from here.

                    FEMALE RELATIVE 1
We live near the West Bank of the Nile.

MARYAM hands JESUS over the MALE RELATIVE 1 as everyone begins walking, talking and smiling along the way.

INT. APARTMENT – NIGHT

MARYAM sits in her well furnished apartment with a FEMALE RELATIVE 2 (30). Baby Jesus is sleep in a wooden cradle.

                    FEMALE RELATIVE 2
          So how is IMRAN doing?

                    MARYAM
          By the grace of God, he is doing well.

                    FEMALE RELATIVE
          We hope he comes to visit us soon.

                    MARYAM
          He will.
               (looks at baby Jesus)
          So how are things here in Cairo?

                    FEMALE RELATIVE 1
          The Romans and Greeks now rule over our
          people. Our grain is grown to feed Rome.
          Our land has been confiscated. So we live in
          various quarters among our own kind. In
          this way, we are mostly safe.

                    MARYAM
          Well JESUS and I will reside here among
          his own people where it will be safe and
          sound.

                    MALE RELATIVE 2
               (stand up)
          Your right. Now get some rest MARYAM.
          We will see you and the baby in a few days.

                                        DISSOLVE:

EXT. CLASSROOM – DAY

FADE IN:

SUPERIMPOSE: FIVE YEARS LATER

JESUS sits on Persian rug among other male STUDENTS. The TEACHER (21), black Nubian female, cute, slant eyes, high cheek bones, green head rap and garment poses a question to STUDENTS. She ask, "what is 10 time 10". JESUS raises his left hand. The TEACHER points at him.

                        JESUS
10 times 10 equals 100.

                        TEACER
Okay, what is 7 times 7?

                        JESUS
                   (raises hand)
49

                        TEACHER
What is 9 time 12?

                        JESUS
                   (raises hand)
108

                        TEACHER
Very good JESUS.

The other STUDENTS look upon JESUS in awe.

                        TEACHER (cont')
JESUS has your mother been helping you
study your math problems?

                        JESUS
Yes maim. And my cousins too.

                        TEACHER
FINE.
                   (beat)
Students, next week we will begin learning
to speak Greek. So get ready.

                        STUDENT 1
                   (loud voice)
Why?

                        JESUS
Yes, why?

                        ALL STUDENTS
                   (whining tone)
Whyyyyyyy?

                        TEACHER (O.S.)
Please calm down class. Later in your
studies, you will learn why. But for now,
know this: When Alexander the Great

conquered Egypt in 332 BC, common Greek
was introduced into our ancient civilization.
So we must learn the language.

CLOSE UP:

All student faces grow with righteous indignation and dissatisfaction.

                TEACHER (cont')
              (looking at students)
Don't worry. You will be alright. I will teach
you well.

                            FADE OUT:

EXT. NILE RIVER – NOON

JESUS and his THREE COUSINS splash and play on the edges of the Nile River. The Sun
is beaming brightly in the sky. MARYAM walks up on the edge of the river. She calls out,
"JESUS, it's time to come home. I have prepared a nice meal for you and COUSINS".

                    JESUS
Okay mother. We are on our way.

The boys run out of the river. As they race by MARAYAM to the apartment, joy and
laugher is expressed in their faces and body movements.

INT. APARTMENT – EVENING

MARYAM, JESUS and his THREE COUSINS (6 – 9) sit at dining table. In the center of the
table is fish, flat bread, brown rice, dates and a jug of milk.

                   COUSIN 1
              (smiling)
Sister MARYAM, this food is hmmm
good!

JESUS and two other COUSINS chomp down on the food.

                   MARYAM
              (looking at cousins)
Praise God. Eat as much as you can.
              (beat)
By the way, I spoke with your uncle. He
will allow you all to sleep over, but
remember to complete your studies
before bedtime.

COUSIN 3
(elated)
YES maim!

MARYAM gets up from the table. She walks to the front door and steps outside to look at the night sky. She sees billions of stars and smiles.

FADE TO BLACK:

INT. CLASSROOM – Day

FADE IN:

SUPERIMPOSE: SEVEN YEARS LATER 6 AD

JESUS (12), 5'6', 120 pounds, black skin, course hair walks around classroom assisting a classmate with math problems. In the b.g., the TEACHER (45), brown skin, tall and slim, clean shaven face, bald head is aiding a group of students standing around a table.

NARRATOR (V.O.)
JESUS was a very intelligent student. His
mother enrolled into school when he was
five years old. Throughout his educational
career, he took astronomy, geometry courses
in the branch of science. By the age of twelve
he was advanced and ready to finished
school.

INT. DESERT – NIGHT

Twelve OLD MEN black men, brown, red skin sit in a circle around a lit camp fire sipping on tea. Each OLD MAN sit on their own Persian rugs. At a distance, are several tents and twelve camels.

OLD MAN 1
(announces to group)
The child has come of age. He is living
in Cairo, Egypt with his mother. The
enemy is going to seek to destroy him
at some point of his life. He will be the
last prophet sent to the Jews is written
in our ancient scripts.

OLD MAN 2
(stands, calmly speaks)
Then I must go to find him at all cost. I
will teach the boy the science tuning in
into the thinking of those who shall seek
to kill him.

OLD MAN 2 calmly stands up and walks over to his camel. He mounts the camel and rides off in the night of the desert.

FADE OUT:

EXT. EGYPT – STREET CORNER - DAY

OLD MAN 2 stands on a road near the school where JESUS attends. He sees JESUS, the youngest of his classmates walking out the school building door with twelve other BOYS (14 – 16). They all walk into a crowd of people and disappear from the sight of the OLD MAN. The old man thinks to himself, "Oh darn, I will come back tomorrow and get in his path."

FADE OUT:

EXT. FABRIC STOREFRONT – DAY

SUPERIMPOSE: NEXT DAY

The OLD MAN purchases some silk fabric and places it over his shoulder. He walks outside the storefront. He looks toward the school building and sees JESUS walking on a path with one STUDENT. The OLD MAN walks on the same path and stops to ask a group of other BOYS a question who were standing near JESUS.

> NARRATOR (V.O.)
> The next day, the OLD MAN saw JESUS
> and a CLASSMATE walking alone. JESUS
> was talking about his lessons and was
> teaching his CLASSMATE algebra.
>
> The OLD MAN pretended he was looking
> for a certain street number and JESUS
> overheard him asking a group of BOYS
> nearby.
>
> OLD MAN
> (talking loud)
> Excuse me, would any of you boys know
> where 1931 Hopi is located?
>
> BOY 1
> What is the number?
>
> OLD MAN
> (speaking loud)
> One-Nine-Three-One 1931 Hopi.
>
> JESUS
> (looks to his left side)
> Oh, I know where you want to go. Just

follow me. It's only a few doors from
where I live.

The OLD MAN looks at JESUS. Then he looks back at the BOYS. He says, "thank you
young men. Have a good day." The group of BOYS say, "Shylamah" and walk down the
crowded street toward the market place.

JESUS'S CLASSMATE shakes his hand and runs off to catch to the groups of BOYS.
JESUS and the OLD MAN stand alone, looking at one another.

> OLD MAN
> (slightly smiles)
> I heard you talking about algebra. You
> are a very smart boy. I have a grandson
> and he is studying the same course. I
> would like for you to come over and
> teach his lesson as you could help him
> a lot.
> (beat)
> Can you help him?

> JESUS
> I will. I enjoy teaching people.

JESUS and OLD MAN begin to slowly walk down the street. The OLD MAN walks in
stride. His arms lowered behind his back, right hand clinching the left hand.

> OLD MAN
> Do you know who you are and what your
> name is?

> JESUS
> Yes, my name is EASHUA, and I don't know
> more than that.
> (beat)
> But, I believe that I will be a great man
> someday.

> OLD MAN
> Yes, your name is in the Quran. Haven't you
> seen it there?

JESUS looks puzzled at the OLD MAN. He squints his eyes, looks up above the OLD
MAN'S right shoulder and sees a hawk soring in a circular motion in the sky.

> OLD MAN (cont')
> (taps jesus arm)
> You are that man. I am not looking for a
> number. I was looking for you.

JESUS intensely listens to every word spoken by the OLD MAN.

> OLD MAN (cont')
> I have something that I want to teach
> you because as soon a you finish school,
> you will leave home and you are going to
> Europe to the Adamic Civilization to teach.
> You must know how to take care of
> yourself because they will try to kill you.

FADE OUT:

INT. APARTMMENT FRONT DOOR – LATE EVENING

MARYAM standing outside her apartment front door talking with several RELATIVES. She sees JESUS walking up the street with his MALE RELATIVE 1. They are holding hands like friends and laughing.

CUT TO:

INT. BEDROOM – NIGHT

JESUS lay in his bed staring at the oil lamp. MARYAM walks into his room.

> MARYAM
> (concerned)
> You came home very late this evening.

> JESUS
> (sits up in his bed)
> I sorry, but Mother, I met this old man
> and he was telling me something about
> my future.

MARYAM sits down in a corner chair in JESUS'S bedroom.

> MARYAM
> What did he say sweetheart?

BEGIN FLASHBACK:

OLD MAN looking down at JESUS. JESUS looking up at the OLD MAN. The OLD MAN sets his hand on JESUS'S shoulder.

> OLD MAN
> Your name is in the Quran. When you
> finish school, you will leave Egypt to
> begin your mission. You will be the
> last prophet sent to the Adamic
> civilization of Europe. They will seek

to kill you. But I am going to help you
protect yourself from those who will
seek to hurt you.

BACK TO PRESENT

MARYAM standing up with her back turned to JESUS as she listens. She is looking out
bedroom window.

                    MARYAM
Where is this old man?

                    JESUS
I don't know.

                    MARYAM
What do you mean you don't know?

                    YUSEF
He just came out of nowhere. He had
such a beautiful concerning spirit for
my well-being. His garments where
all white and clean.

MARYAM quietly walks over to JESUS. She leans over and hugs him tightly. He hugs her
tightly in return.

                    MARYAM
              (whispers in his ear)
It's all true son. You do have a divine
mission ahead of you.

JESUS lays back in the bed and says, "Is the old man my father?"

                    MARYAM (cont')
No son, you are JESUS son of YUSEF. Your
father is from an ancient line of the kings
who built the ancient city of Jebus centuries
before the invasion by foreigners.

                    JESUS
You mean Jerusalem?

                    MARYAM
Yes JESUS. Before the foreign invaders,
our land was truly peaceful.

                    JESUS
              (looking into maryam's
              eyes)
         When may I meet my father?

                   MARYAM
         One day you shall meet him. Now go to
         sleep my beloved E-SHO.

JESUS smiles. MARYAM kisses him on the forehead. She walks out of the bedroom. JESUS thinks to himself, "wow!" as he stares at the ceiling with a smile. Then he closes his eyes and falls to sleep.

                                        FADE TO BLACK:

EXT. STOREFRONT – DAY

FADE IN:

The OLD MAN mettles around a storefront. He looks up and he sees JESUS walking behind his classmates. When JESUS walked by the storefront, the OLD MAN walks up to him.

                   OLD MAN
              (smiling brightly)
         Shylamah brother EASHUA!

                    JESUS
              (smiling brightly)
         Shylamah old man!

                   OLD MAN
         May I walk along with you?

                    JESUS
         Sure, I am on my way home to my
         mothers apartment.

The OLD MAN and JESUS divert along a quite pathway. They walk, talk and stop several times. The OLD MANS hands and arms gesticulate around his head, his heart and ears. JESUS is repeating the movements made by the OLD MAN.

                  NARRATOR (V.O.)
         The OLD MAN finally gets JESUS alone
         and begins teaching him how to tune into
         the thinking of his enemies to avoid being
         captured.

         This ancient science is called radio in the
         head that enables a person to receive and

send messages using the mind and heart.
It was easy for JESUS to learn anything.
He learned in three days because JESUS
was good at math.

JESUS and OLD MAN stop walking. In the f.g., MARYAM and several people stand and talk in front of the corner bakery.

                    OLD MAN
                (looking at JESUS)
        Now you can go anywhere you want to
        go. You can take care of yourself...
                    (beat)
        nobody can harm you unless you let them.

                                        DISSOLVE:

INT. SCHOOL COURT YARD – DAY

FADE IN:

All the mothers of the students fill into school courtyard. They stand on the south wall. Thirteen male students sit on Persian rugs, in two rows, on the north wall. JESUS is sitting on the far right side, second row. The light of the sun beams through the open roof courtyard beaming upon JESUS'S beautiful black skin.

In walks four elderly SCHOLARS. Three are females and one is a male. They all stand behind the students.

                    FEMALE 1
        Welcome parents to our graduation
        ceremony. Today these thirteen
        students have completed their courses
        of study at our educational institution.

                    FEMALE 2
        A special acknowledgement goes out to
        JESUS. He is merely twelve years of age,
        and has completed all our courses in
        record time.
                    (beat)
        Please give him a hand.

Parents and students alike clap their hands. JESUS stands up, look at his mother. He takes a bow and sits down.

                                        FADE OUT:

INT. HOPI STREET - EVENING

All of JESUS'S relatives and friends enjoy a festive cookout in their quarters. Food is plentiful. Little children are running around playing and laughing. JESUS performs a traditional dance along with other males. The females observe and clap to the rhythm of the drum beats, flutes and string instruments.

In the b.g., two pretty mixed Egyptian YOUNG LADIES (16), light brown skin, black long silky wavy hair, black pupils see the men performing their traditional dance.

                    TOMASSA
          Oh, look MARTA let's get closer.

                    MARTA
          Okay, lets go.

As MARTA and TOMASSA run closer to look at the dancing men, MARTA zooms in on JESUS'S everything move. He appears to move in slow motion. JESUS has a big smile on his face, eyes closed.

                                        DISSOLVE:

EXT. TEA SHOP – EARLY MORNING

FADE IN:

JESUS (14) and MARYAM sit in tea shop sipping tea and eating sweet bread.

                    JESUS
          Mother I'm so proud of you.

                    MARYAM
          Why, son.

                    JESUS
          You sponsored that entire event yesterday
          for the community.

                    MARYAM
          Oh know son, your father helped me pay
          for everything. It was your graduation
          gift.

                    JESUS
                    (elated)
          He did?

                    MARYAM
                    (smiling)
          Yes, he has a very successful carpentry

business now. Most of this work is in
Jerusalem.

                    JESUS
               (smiling)
Wow!
               (beat)
Mother, I must tell you something.

                    MARYAM
What is it E-SHO?

                    JESUS
I am going to South Europe.

                    MARYAM
               (distressed)
But son, you are only twelve years old.

                    JESUS
I can't help it, but the spirit is moving
me to teach those people down there.
Perhaps they shall change their wicked
ways.

MARYAM looks sad. She places her hand on JESUS hand staring at his profile as he
gazes out the window of the tea shop.

                                             FADE OUT:

INT. EGYPTIAN TEMPLE – EDGE OF LAKE - DAY

JESUS, wearing a white garment sits on a granite bench inside an Egyptian Temple in
front of a granite stone slab. On the walls of the Temple are ancient pictographs of black
men and women.

Standing in front of JESUS are TWELVE PREIST (85), all dressed in white robes, white
turbans, grey beards, brown and black skin. Each PREIST walks by and places one
papyrus scroll on the granite stone slab in front of JESUS.

                    PREIST 1
               (pauses at table)
My son, you were brought to this
ancient Temple of Kerma to review
a few pages of old Testament scrolls.
These pages shall guide you on your
journey.

JESUS stands to his feet. He looks over at the other eleven PREIST. Then he sits back on
the granite slab.

PREIST 1 (cont')
These scrolls contain, God knowledge,
logic, reason and future prophecies to
come. They represent the best of what
prophet Moses, Jeremiah, Isaiah and
others revealed to the house of Israel
2,000 years from our current era.

JESUS
(looking at walls and ceiling)
I'm curious.
(beat)
When was this Temple built in Kerma?

PRIEST 1
(smiling)
Thousands of years ago, son.

The PRIEST begin to walk out of the TEMPLE. In the b.g., JESUS opens the scrolls and
begins reading page after page.

FADE OUT:

INT. APARTMENT – NIGHT

INRAM, full grey beard, and MARYAM sit in her apartment by the front window. I nice
breeze blows through the curtains.

IMRAN
(quiet tone)
So how is my grandson?

MARYAM
(sad tone)
He is planning to go to South Europe.

IMRAN
Has he let yet?

MARYAM
Not, yet. I have tried to give him
everything to prevent him from leaving.

IMRAN
Where is he now?

MARYAM
Lately he has been traveling back and
forth down into Nubia studying.

            IMRAN
Well their nothing we can do to hold
him back. The divine spirit is upon him.
        (beat)
His life and death is written in the book
as is yours and mine.

IMRAN grabs his daughter's hand. They both look up at the stars twinkle and sparkle
as the wind blows the curtains wide open.

EXT. BOAT – MORNING

JESUS and SCHOLAR PRIEST 1 stand aft atop a boat riding up the Nile River. He and
JESUS are dressed brown garments and white turbans.

From a distance, to the right of the boat, the shoreline bustles with Romeo-Greek patrons
and merchants, dressed in Egyptian attire. Roman soldiers stand guard on the merchant
shop and Greek style Temples gleaming on hillsides. Poorly dressed slaves of many
ethnic backgrounds work on a hillside breaking stones.

            JESUS
        (looking on shoreline)
Where are all these foreigners coming
from?

            PREIST 1 (O.S.)
They are Romeo-Greeks, descendants of
those whom conquered our lands. These
are the people of South Europe.
        (beat)
Have you learned to speak their language?

            JESUS
Very well my brother sir, very well.

JESUS continues looking on shoreline with distain. The boat glides by a seaport. He
sees hundreds of black men, poorly dressed carrying bags of grain over their shoulders
onto Roman ships.

            PRIEST 1
        (looks at JESUS)
You see JESUS, our divine land now
serves as Rome's grain house. Their
ultimate goal is the build their
civilization on the backs of our people.
Now tell me what have learned so far.

            JESUS
So these are people whom the scrolls
refer to as the Adamic race?

The PRIEST looks at JESUS with a slight smile, he says, "So you have learned well my son." JESUS looks more determined than ever.

DISSOVLE:

INT. TEA SHOP – MORNING

FADE IN

SUPERIMPOSE: TWO YEARS LATER

JESUS (14) walks through the door of tea shop. He 5'6', 120 lbs. looking very fit. Upon seeing him enter, MARYAM jumps up from her chair. She runs over toward him. They both hung one another with tears in eyes, smiling.

                    MARYAM
          Come, come, sit down my son.

JESUS walks to a table with his mother. They sit down. He notices the tea shop is much larger with customers walking in and out buying flesh baked goods.

                    MARYAM (cont')
          Oh I miss you so much. It's been two
          years.

                    JESUS
          I miss you too Mother. Wow, mother, the
          shop is much larger when I was last
          here.

                    MARYAM
          I expanded the size when I bought it from
          your cousin.

                    JESUS
          Nice.

                    MARYAM
          So tell me my son, how it feel to be fourteen
          years old?

                    JESUS
               (talking strong)
          I feel wiser than ever before. I traveled all the
          way down to the where the Nile begins and
          back up to where it ends on the Mediterranean
          Sea. I saw our people serving our oppressors
          carrying grains of wheat onto Roman ships.

PEOPLE in the tea shop begin crowding around the table to listen to JESUS speak.

JESUS (cont')
But this too shall come to an end! Thus saith
the lord our fathers.

PEOPLE 1
The boy speaks to truth!

PEOPLE 2 (Women)
He speaks what has been in our hearts
for centuries!

The PEOPLE in the tea shop begin shouting, "praise God for this child, praise God! Alleluiah!" Several men walk up to JESUS and shake his hand. The women look on with tears in their eyes.

CUT TO:

EXT. LIVING ROOM – MORNING

MARYAM is wearing all white garb and hair piece. She stands by the window looking outside. JESUS walks out of his bedroom. He is wearing shoulder bag. The room is completely silent he walks over to his mother. She firmly looks at him and hands him a leather pouch of coins.

MARYAM
Here is two thousand dollars, son. You
may need it on your journey. I connected
you father to meet you in Jerusalem. For
too knows your name indeed is in the
book.

JESUS kisses his mother on the forehead. He walks out the door. MARYAM walks over to the window and peaks out. She watches her son walk two blocks handing out money (gold coins) from the pouch she give him. She smiles and cries at the same time.

FADE OUT:

INSERT MAP TRAVEL SEQUENCE FROM CAIRO TO JERUSALEM, TOWARD TO SOUTH EUROPE VIA ANTIOCH, TARSUS TO PERGA:

NARRATOR (V.O.)
JESUS leaves Cairo, EGYPT on a fast mail
camel to Jerusalem where he meets his
father, YUSEF at the camel station in
Jerusalem. They give each other a strong
embrace. JESUS gives YUSEF his leather
sandals.

From Jerusalem, he begins his 600 mile
journey walking near the coastlines to

South Europe bare feet teaching as he traveled. If he got hungry, he would not eat your bread unless you let him work for it. He would wash his own clothes in a lake or someplace where he could find water.

JESUS had a hard time trying to teach Freedom, Justice, Equality to members of the Adamic Civilization. Nevertheless, he taught anywhere and everywhere that he could get the people to listen to him.

EXT. APPLE ORCHARD – DAY

SUPERIMPOSE: GREEK CITY OF PERGA

JESUS is standing under an apple tree. Fourteen FIELD WORKERS (7 women and 7 men ages 14 to 45), pale and olive tone, black hair are gathering around him. He gestures for everyone to sit down.

> JESUS
> Tell me, what town is this?

> FIELD WORKER 1
> You don't know where you are?

> JESUS
> I am on a journey.

> FIELD WORKER 2
> You are in the city of Perga. What kind of Journey do you mean young man?

> JESUS
> I am on a journey to teach freedom, justice and equality to all whom will listen. My name is EASHUA.

> FIELD WORKER 2
> That is Jesus in Greek.

> JESUS
> Yes, JESUS in Greek. But EASHUA in my mother tongue or Aramaic.

> FIELD WORKER 3
> Well JESUS, our Roman master will punish us if we sit here too long. So, what is it that you want to teach us?

>   JESUS
> Blessed are the poor in spirit, for theirs
> is the kingdom of heaven. Blessed are
> they who mourn, for they shall be
> comforted. Blessed are they who hunger
> and thirst for righteousness, for they
> shall be satisfied. Blessed are the pure
> of heart, for they shall see God. Blessed
> are they who are persecuted for the sake
> of righteousness, for theirs is the
> kingdom of heaven.

FIELD WORKER 1 stands up. In the f.g., she sees the ROMAN PATRICIAN riding a horse heading their way.

>   FIELD WORKER 1
>   (panick mode)
> Everyone stand to your feet, he's coming!

JESUS looks over his shoulder. He says to everyone, "calm down, all is well." ROMAN PATRICIAN dismounts his horse several feet away from JESUS.

>   ROMAN PATRICIAN
>   (authoritative)
> Who are you and what are you doing
> among my servants?

FIELD WORKERS begin to slowly disperse back to their working areas leaving JESUS alone with the ROMAN PATRICIAN. FIELD WORKER 3 is talking to FIELD WORKER 2 as they pick apple from a tree placing them in baskets. In the b.g., JESUS and ROMAN PATRICIAN standoff face to face.

>   FIELD WORKER 3
> What did he mean by 'saying for the sake
> of righteousness?
>   (beat)
> There is no such thing a right or wrong.

>   FIELD WORKER 2
> That's right. We live as Greeks and Romans
> live. The angel Artemis watches over us.

FIELD WORKER 2 turns arounds. He sees the ROMAN PATRICIAN and JESUS siting down beneath apple tree facing one another. They appear to be conversing. Suddenly, JESUS stands to his feet and says, "as a man thinketh, so is he." Then he walks away. The ROMAN PATRICIAN lays back on the grass, folds his arms behind his head and closes his eyes.

                                                              FADE OUT:

INSERT MAP TRAVEL SEQUENCE FROM PAMPHYLIA TO PERGA TO EUROMOS TO EPHESUS:

NARRATOR (V.O.)
JESUS continues to journey deeper miles
into South Europe. Along the highways
and byways he sees people in utter poverty,
physical deformities, skin deceases, and
living in uncleanliness. He would spend
nearly two years in many villages teaching
basic morals and cleanliness. His oft-
repeated message was 'as a man thinketh
in his heart, so is he'.

EXT. VILLAGE – EVENING

SUPERIMPOSE: VILLAGE OF PAMPHYLIA

JESUS walks through the forest. He uses a wooden staff to beat back the brushes. As he walks forward, he hears a faint sound of music and laughter. He approaches a clearance area from the forest and sees a mass of all tribes of people, light red, yellow, brown and pale white dancing wildly, hugging and kissing one another. When he steps out of the forest from behind the bushes, the party stopped. A half nude FEMALE walks over to JESUS.

FEMALE
(flirtatious)
Now who is this dark and handsome?

JESUS
My name is EASHUA.

The FEMALE begins to rub on the right arm of JESUS. Then a MALE from among the crowd walks over the JESUS.

JESUS
Why are you people not fully dressed?

MALE
(jolly)
We are celebrating our sex god Aphrodite.
Remove your clothes and join us my
friend.

The music starts up again. The people begin to dance freakishly. They drunk from wine and other vice. JESUS stands firm holding his wooden staff with both hands. Then he says, "I did not come here to dance and party, I came here to teach righteousness."

FEMALE
Is that going to ruin our celebration in the
name of our goddess of love and beauty?

MALE
If so, we don't want to hear your teachings
about what you say is right or wrong.

JESUS continues to stand firmly in place. In the b.g., he sees the lust in the eyes of the
people. The music is getting louder and louder. He kicks the dust off his feet and says,
"I know your thoughts." Then he backs away into the forest.

FADE TO BLACK:

EXT. LAKE – FORREST - DAY

FADE IN:

JESUS bathes in a cove on a lake. Birds are singing. The warm rays of the sun above beam
down through the trees. His clothes hang from a tree branch on the edge of the river
bank. The thick forestry of trees provide cover for him from being seen.

DISSOLVE:

EXT. STREETS OF EPHESUS - MORNING

SUPERIMPOSE: EIGHTEEN YEARS LATER CITY OF EPHESUS

JESUS (31), thinly shaded black beard growing down the side of his jawbone under his
chin. No mustache and tightly coiled short black hair on his head enters the city of
EPHESUS. He walks and marvels at its polished stone Greek style buildings, polished
stone streets and several public baths. He sees on grape vineyards and olive trees
growing on the hillsides. The people dressed in Greek Togas. JESUS stops an old man to
ask, "Where is the nearest Synagogue? The old man simply points down the street which
is lined up with Roman soldiers every other corner.

EXT. JEWISH MERCHANT KIOSK - DAY

JESUS walks over to a Kiosk manned by two JEWS (25) dressed in in Greek Togas, wearing
star of David bracelets, clean shaven face, black hair and blue eyes. On their Kiosk stand
are neatly placed precious stones.

JESUS
Shalom!

JEW 1
We don't speak Hebrew, we are Greek
speakers.

                         JEW 2
                        (cocky)
                Who are you anyway?
                         JESUS
                By whose authority do you ask?

                         JEW 1
                     (caught off guard)
                I am AGAPIOS.

                         JEW 2
                I am KADMOS. What do you need of us?

                         JESUS
                I would like to speak with your Rabbi's.

                         JEW 1
                And what is it that you like to say?

                         JESUS
                Tell them I did not come to change the
                law of Moses, but to full it as contrasted
                with what was expected.

The two JEWS looked at one another. Then looked at JESUS and said, "one moment."

INT. INSIDE LUXIOUS HOME – EVENING

Five RABBI'S, (ages 55 – 70), grey long bushy beards, traditional Jewish costumes and head coverings sit on chairs and couches in a luxurious home built on the edge of a hill top. JESUS is walked out of house onto the marble deck by two scantly dress women.

                         RABBI 1
                    (whispers to RABBI 2)
                He looks Ethiopian or Nubian.

                         RABBI 2
                      (whispers)
                He could be of Jebusite descent.

RABBI 2 beckons JESUS to come over to join him and the other RABBI'S. He walks over bare foot and sits in a seat slightly off to the side where the RABBI'S are sitting. His chair was situated overlooking the beautiful city of EPHESUS.

                         RABBI 2
                      (clears throat)
                Shalom.

JESUS
(Shalom) Rabbi

RABBI 1
(left eye brow up)
So you want to speak with us, where
were you born?

JESUS
I was born in Palestine.

RABBI 1
Who is your mother?

JESUS
MARYAM of Bethlehem

RABBI 2
Who is your father?

JESUS
That is not what I come to talk about.

RABBI 2
Yes, yes; of course.

RABBI 3 whispers to RABBI 4, is he a bastard child?

JESUS
Why have you wise men of Israel mixed
what prophet Moses revealed to you
with Greek Hellenism? I have come out
of Egypt, and traveled 600 miles into
the city of EPHESUS and see no marks of
what Moses revealed for your people?

RABBI 9
Our people fought gallantly to established
our own independence under Roman rule-

JESUS
(interrupts)
-Did you side with Mattathias the Hasmonean
prince during the Maccabee revolt against
Hellenism?

RABBI 9
We are allies with Rome. For this, we have
riches and independence as a Roman client
state. We are wealthy Ephesians. Look around,

our homes are decorated with beautiful
frescoes and mosaics. We live in luxurious
houses on this hill with many bedrooms,
triclinium, and kitchens. Do you wish to see
us lose it?

                    JESUS
For the pagans pursue all these things, and
your Heavenly Father knows that you need
them. But seek first the kingdom of God
and His righteousness, and all these things
will be added unto you.
                    (beat)
What I come to teach gives independence for
evermore. I teach, freedom, justice and
equality. What I have discovered through my
journey here is thievery, syncretism and
paganism.

JESUS points at naked Greek statues on the edges of the deck. They turn around.

                    JESUS (cont')
Woe to you Scribes and Pharisees, pretenders,
and hypocrites! You keep locking people out
of the kingdom of heaven! For you neither
enter nor permit those trying to enter to go in.

                    RABBI 3
                    (stands to his feet in anger)
How dare you question are motives you black
bastard!

                    JESUS
As a man thinketh, so is he.

                    RABBIA 4
At least we were not born of fornication!

RABBI 2 intervenes by shouting, "quite?" He looks at JESUS and says, "will you excuse
us for a moment?" All the RABBI'S, except RABBI 1, stand up and walk over to a corner
on the deck. JESUS turns his head slightly to the right, eyes slanted downward. He
hears a ring sound in his right ear. Then he hears running footsteps and armor
clanging.

                    JESUS
                    (looks at rabbi 1)
Pardon me, where is the latrine?

RABBI 1 one points to the side of the house. JESUS gets up and walks in that direction.

                                                            CUT TO:

EXT. ROMAN OFFICERS – LATE EVENING

Several ROMAN OFFICERS ride in chariots down the streets of EPHESUS.

EXT. HILL TOP – NIGHT

JESUS running up a path through the hill tops of EPHESUS. He reaches an enclosed bushy area. He stops to take several deep breaths before sitting down leaning his back against a cedar tree rubbing his sore feet. Then he closes his eyes and falls asleep.

FADE TO BLACK:

EXT. CARGO SHIP – DAY

SUPERIMPOSE – PORT CITY OF LYCIA

JESUS disembarks a cargo ship. He is carrying a bag of grain on his back along with other men. Each man drops a bag of grain onto a scaled on the dock. A roman PAYMASTER stands by handing each man two cooper coins. JESUS reaches the PAYMASTER, drops his bag on the scale. The paymaster looks down at JESUS, places two copper coins into his hand.

INSERT COIN – ON THE FACE OF COIN IS CESARE AUGUSTUS OF ROME. WRITTEN ON COIN ARE THE WORDS, 'DIVINE RULER OF ROME':

PAYMASTER
Welcome to the Port City of Lycia.

JESUS looks up and says, "thanks". Then he drops the coin in the pouch given to him by his mother and heads down the boardwalk. He sees drunken men and women stumbling around; laughing. Men kissing men, women kissing women. From a distance, he sees a sign on a building reading, "Rooms for Rent."

INT. ROOM – NIGHT

JESUS lays on a bed in a small room. He hears to voice of MARYAM in his right ear, "how are you my son". He smiles, closes his eyes and falls to sleep.

FADE OUT:

EXT. MERCHANT STORE – MORNING

JESUS stands on corner near a merchant fruit stand. He is speaking. Seven PEOPLE crowd around him. Four are dressed in the finest Greek clothing. One is a WEALTHY WOMEN. She has two European servants standing behind him, heads hanging down.

JESUS
(looking very pleasant
at two servants)
Lend me your ear brothers and sisters.

The WEALTHY WOMEN lightly taps her two servants with a switch and says, "pay attention, you learn something." The other PEOPLE curiously stand by and lean forward as JESUS begins to speak.

> JESUS (cont')
> There was a rich man whose manager
> was accused of wasting his possessions.
> So he called him in and asked him, 'What
> is this I hear about you? Give an account
> of your management, because you cannot
> be manager any longer.' "The manager
> said to himself, 'What shall I do now? My
> master is taking away my job. I'm not
> strong enough to dig, and I'm ashamed
> to beg— I know what I'll do so that, when
> I lose my job here, people will welcome
> me into their houses.'

TWO servants look at JESUS more closely.

> JESUS (cont')
> (animated)
> "So he called in each one of his master's
> debtors. He asked the first, 'How much do
> you owe my master?' "'Nine hundred
> gallons of olive oil,' he replied. "The
> manager told him, 'Take your bill, sit down
> quickly, and make it four hundred and fifty.'
> "Then he asked the second, 'And how much
> do you owe?' "'A thousand bushels of wheat,'
> he replied. "He told him, 'Take your bill and
> make it eight hundred.'

> WEALTHY WOMEN
> Hey, how are you trying to influence my two
> servants. Are you a trouble maker?

> JESUS
> By no means! I am a teacher of freedom,
> justice, equality. The master commended
> the dishonest manager because he had
> acted shrewdly.
>
> For the people of this world are more
> shrewd in dealing with their own kind
> than are the people of the light. I tell you,
> use worldly wealth to gain friends for
> yourselves, so that when it is gone, you
> will be welcomed into eternal dwellings.

JESUS takes two steps back, looks at the WEALTHY WOMEN and walks away.

                    WEALTHY WOMEN
                        (frowning)
              Hey, come here! Who are you?

WEALTHY WOMEN looks at four other people and says, "did you hear how that man insulted me?

                       PEOPLE 1
              What I heard was how we should treat
              one another.

Other three PEOPLE shake their heads in agreement. WEALTHY WOMEN looks at all Four PEOPLE with distain. Makes a huffing sound before storming off with her two servant trailing behind periodically turning their heads back toward the four other PEOPLE.

EXT. STONE MILL GRINDER – DAY

The WEALTHY WOMEN'S two SERVANTS grind mill outside a barn. Goats are running around the barn.

                      SERVANT ONE
              That Ethiopian man was telling the truth.

                      SERVANT TWO
              He spoke in parables. I believe it was meant
              for our master.

                      SERVANT ONE
              I believe so. She is very shrewd-

                      SERVANT TWO
              -I think that man is one of the people of the
              light. I wish I could follow type of person
              away from being a servant.

Both SERVANTS stop grinding mill. They tip toe to the other side of the barn. In the f.g., the see rows of olive trees their master talking with three ROMAN SOLDIERS in front of the WEALTHY WOMEN'S luxurious cottage home.

                     ROMAN SOLDIER
              The person whom you described sounds like
              the person we have been after for some time
              now.

                    WEALTHY WOMEN
              I hope you check him soon!

                                        FADE OUT:

EXT. DESSERT FIELD – NOON

SUPERIMPOSE: ALEXANDRIA, EGPYT

Several hundred reddish-brown Egyptian men sit in a field of sand in rows of twenty. Standing before them is GERMANICUS, the nephew of Tiberius Caesar flacked by thirty-six armed Roman soldiers. GERMANICUS is wearing his official roman attire addressing the Egyptian men. In the b.g., is the glorious city of Alexandria.

> GERMANICUS
> To my fellow men of Egypt. You are now
> subjects of Rome. The Ptolemaic Dynasty
> is no more. If you desire to become citizens
> under Roman rule, you must register in
> Alexandria and join the Roman Army.

GERMANICUS pauses. He grabs the pennant around his neck with his left hand. The Egyptian men sitting closet to GERMANICUS look hypnotized staring at the pennant hanging around his neck.

CAMERA ZOOM IN:

CLOSE UP:

DEPICTION OF THE ROMAN EGYPTIAN GOD, SERAPIS HANGING AROUND NECK OF GERMANICUS

FADE OUT:

INT. BYWAY ROADSIDE – HOME – EVENING

SUPERIMPOSE: ONE MONTH LATER

JESUS stands in front of a water hole answering questions to an audience of twenty-one GREEKS dressed poorly, messy hair; some have sores covering their bodies. A certain person among the group slips from the gathering. He runs off into the bushes. JESUS notices him leaving, but continues teaching his congregation.

> GREEK 1
> Why do you teach in parables, Jesus?

> JESUS
> I know that I am speaking to people who
> don't love the truth more that sin.

> JEWISH 3 (Women)
> Well I bought this omelet during Passover
> some time ago from a Temple priest. He
> said wear it to remove all my sins.

JEW 1
Jesus, do you love the truth?

JESUS
I am the truth. As I man thinketh, so is
he.

GREEK 5
Now that sounds really arrogant.

JESUS
Consider this. There was a certain rich
man, which was clothed in purple and
fine linen, and fared sumptuously every
day: And there was a certain beggar,
which was laid at his gate, full of sores,
And desiring to be fed with the crumbs
which fell from the rich man's table:
moreover the dogs came and licked his
sores.

And it came to pass, that the beggar died,
and was carried by the angels into
Abraham's bosom: the rich man also died,
and was buried; And in hell he lift up his
eyes, being in torments, and seeth
Abraham afar off, and the beggar in his
bosom. And he cried and said, Father
Abraham, have mercy on me, and send the
beggar, that he may dip the tip of his finger
in water, and cool my tongue; for I am
tormented in this flame.

GREEK (Boy)
Who is the Moses and Abraham? I have
never heard of these gods. I know of
Zeus, Apollo, Athena.

JESUS
(looks at boy)
I believe the gentleman that slipped away
earlier can answer that question.

The crowd look around. JESUS slightly turns his head to the right and looks into the
bushes. He closes his eyes. In his right ear, he hears the sound of fast moving
footsteps and clanging metal. He opens his eyes, looks at the gathering and dismisses
them. Then he begins to quickly run away.

EXT. PATHWAY – EVENING

Three Roman soldiers ride horses down a pathway. JESUS has fled. Only three people remain behind (two females and one male) relaxing on the grass. The Roman soldiers dismount their horses yelling, "Where is the trouble maker?" One soldier kicks the male laying in grass. The other soldiers grabbed the two females and drag them off into the bushes.

CUT TO:

EXT. FOREST AREA – NIGHT

JESUS runs through the forest down a bushy pathway. He sees a cavern by a mound of rocks. He heads for the rocks.

INT. INSIDE CAVERAN – NIGHT

JESUS lights a fire with two pieces of flint rocks and dry brush. He looks exhausted as he reaches into a bag grabbing some dry fish and flat bread. He begins eating.

CUT TO:

EXT. ROMAN GYMNASIUM – DAY

SUPERIMPOSE: ROME 19 AD

The great crowd exudes great enthusiasm as they watch multiple wrestling matches of naked men in the massive Roman style gymnasium. In the f.g., midway up the crest shaped gymnasium sits, Cesare TIBERIUS in his VIP seat box area. Seated next to him are several JEWS wearing traditional garments.

JEW 1
TIBERIUS, we Jews identify themselves with Roman politics and exert at times some influence at public meetings. We have maintained constant commercial relations with Rome and pay the Temple tax in Jerusalem. Why have you decided to expel us from Rome?

TIBERIUS
You ask why? Tell me what you have learned about the Roman noblewoman who was swindled by a synagogue. Besides, your people have given Rome so much agitation and revolts in and around Jerusalem. You leave me with no other alternative?

The crowd roars and cheers for the wrestlers in the gymnasium. TIBERIUS looks out at the wrestlers.

66

TIBERIUS
(looks at rabbi)
After all, I am Caesar!

ROMAN OFFICERS enter seating box area. They escort the JEWS out. TIBERIUS stands up to his feet clapping along with hearing the roaring crowds in the gymnasium. The RABBI'S turn for one last look at the gymnasium.

DISSOLVE:

EXT. SAND COVE ON BEACH – MORNING

FADE IN:

SUPERIMPOSE: JEWISH TOWN OF CAESAREA, PALISTINE 30 AD

Small boats sail off the coastline on a bright warm morning. People are swimming in the water, children playing in the sand. From a distance, a woman, high yellow skin notices a crowd of people standing around a black man.

CAMERA ZOOM IN:

CLOSE UP:

JESUS'S black skin radiates with every beam of light from the sun. He is smiling.

JESUS (P.O.V.)
Ask me what you wish.

A crowd of ten JEWISH MEN, four JEWISH WOMEN and seven BROWN SKIN MEN engage JESUS with questions.

BROWN SKIN MAN 1
Is our god upset at us? Is this why there
has been so much death and revolts over
the years.

JEWISH MAN 1
How long will Jewish independence under
Rome endure?

NARRATOR (V.O.)
JESUS put forth another parable saying,
The kingdom of heaven is likened unto a
man which sowed good seed in his field:
But while men slept, his enemy came and
sowed tares among the wheat, and went
his way. But when the blade was sprung
up, and brought forth fruit, then appeared
the tares also. So the servants of the

householder came and said unto him, Sir,
didst not thou sow good seed in thy field
from whence then hath it tares?

A women, her young son and daughter, all high yellow skin walk up after noticing
people in the crowd nervously wrench their hands.

JESUS
An enemy has done this. The servants
said unto him, Will you then that we go
and gather them up? But he said, No;
lest while you gather up the tares, you
root up also the wheat with them. Let
both grow together until the harvest: and
in the time of harvest I will say to the
reapers, gather you together first the tares,
and bind them in bundles to burn them:
but gather the wheat into my barn-

JEWISH MAN 2
(interupts)
-What does that have to do with anything?

JESUS
(looking over the crowd)
There is no avenging God in the sky. This
present civilization will destruct because
of its own evil doings.

JEWISH MAN 2
Ah, I know who your are. Your that trouble
maker!
(beat)
You are the carpenters son?

JESUS
I have from above and you are from below.
Why have you forsaken what prophet Moses
revealed to you?

JEWISH MAN 3
Be mindful what you say Jebusite, I am a
chief priest and he...
(points to man next him)
...is a member of the Sanhedrin? We are
simply enjoying our day at the beach-

                    JESUS
                  (interrupts)
-Here's another parable for you to chew
on.
                  (looks at the sanhedrin)
Have you ever read in the scriptures
wherein it says, 'The stone the builders
rejected has become the cornerstone; the
Lord has done this and it is marvelous in
our eyes'.

Ten olive skin tone MEN walk up behind to where JESUS was teaching. All of them
wearing white robes and wear red fezzes rapped with a white tassel.

                  JESUS (cont')
"Therefore I tell you that the kingdom of
God will be taken away from you and
given to a people who will produce its
fruit. Anyone who falls on this stone will
be broken to pieces; anyone on whom it
falls will be crushed."

                  JEWISH MAN 2
Are you threating to destroy the Temple?

JESUS turns around. He sees the ten olive skin MEN slightly smiling. JESUS slightly
smiles back at them. The chief priest looks at the Sanhedrin judge, wearing black
garment and white head piece. They both look very angry. JESUS walks away down the
sandy beach followed by ten olive skin MEN, including several other people on the
beach.

                  NARRATOR (V.O.)
When the chief priests and the Sanhedrin
judge heard JESUS'S parable, they knew
he was talking about them. They looked
for a way to arrest him, but they were
afraid of the crowd because the people
held that he was a prophet.

                                          FADE OUT:

EXT. SAMARITAN TEMPLE – OUTSIDE – DAY

SUPERIMPOSE: MOUNT GERIZIM

RABBA, his wife and seven other MEN stand with JESUS outside a stone Temple
surrounded by trees. A women hands JESUS a glass of water while the others sip on cups
of tea.

>   RABBA
> So JESUS, your name and teachings is
> spreading.

JESUS chuckles rubbing his hand through his course hair. He says, "I can do nothing about that. I can only imagine how my mother feels". The other Samaritans also laugh.

>   JESUS
> But thank you for allowing me to work
> for the food you feed me.

>   RABBA
> Well, we feel fortunate to have seen you
> yesterday rebuking those Jews.

>   JESUS
> Tell me something RABBA? Why is your
> Temple built outside your village? And
> the other Jews build their synagogues in
> the center of town?

>   RABBA
> I'm more than obliged to give you a brief
> history since I am the elder of my
> community.
>   (beat)
> From what I recall, our Northern Israelitish
> Kingdom here in Jerusalem was transferred
> by our King Omri. He built the city of
> Samaria about 883 B.C. The kingdom
> continued to exist there until it fell before
> Assyria in 722 B.C. Then many of our
> forbearers were deported to various parts
> of Assyria, Babylon. After that period, our
> leaders taught a mixed form of religion,
> partly Israelitish and partly idolatry, hero
> worship, deceased ancestors, fetishism,
> worship of trees, stars and supposed powers
> of nature.

>   JESUS
> In other words, paganized influences have
> overridden the teachings of prophet Moses?

Many other members of the Samaritan community start to gather around to listen to RABBA recite their history.

>   RABBA (cont')
> Yes, but my descendants remained here. We
> have preserved the religion of the ancient

Israelites from before the Babylonian captivity
as opposed to Judaism. Is it related to us, yes,
but as an altered amended religion. We read
from the Torah, they read the Talmud of
Judaism. Thus, hostility remains between us
and the Hellenistic Jews of Jerusalem.

                    JESUS
RABBA you have recalled your peoples
history nearly correct. But you yet do
not know how you were grafted into my
society.

RABBA looks puzzled at JESUS.

                    JESUS
If I may, I will leave you with a parable.

                    RABBA
Certainly.

                    JESUS
A certain man went down from Jerusalem
to Jericho, and fell among thieves, which
stripped him of his raiment, and wounded
him, and departed, leaving him half dead.
And by chance there came down a certain
priest that way: and when he saw him, he
passed by on the other side. And likewise
a Levite, when he was at the place, came
and looked on him, and passed by on the
other side.

But a certain Samaritan, as he journeyed,
came where he was: and when he saw him,
he had compassion on him, And went to
him, and bound up his wounds, pouring in
oil and wine, and set him on his own beast,
and brought him to an inn, and took care
of him. And on the morrow when he
departed, he took out two silver coins, and
gave them to the host, and said unto him,
take care of him; and whatsoever thou
spends more, when I come again, I will
repay thee.

                    RABBA
                  (awe struck)
Beautiful.

                    JESUS
        RABBA thank you for your hospitality. Now I
        must leave to face my destiny.

RABBA walks up to JESUS. He gives him a kiss on his right cheek and his left cheek.
JESUS glances at the faces of the Samaritans gathered behind RABBA. Then JESUS
walks forward. The Samaritans part an opening for him. RABBA watchers JESUS from
behind walking with a limp, feet swollen.

                                            DISSOLVE:

INT. VILLAGE – EVENING

FADE IN:

SUPERIMPOSE: VILIAGE OF BETHANY

JESUS is walks into the village of Bethany. He is walking, with a limp on a wooden staff,
down a narrow street lined small mudbrick homes. The village is occupied by reddish
brown colored men, women and children going about doing their daily task. A women
named MARTA (33), fully dressed, hair scarf, brown eyes sees JESUS limping. She
approaches him.

                    MARTA
            (looking at JESUS'S feet)
        Shylamah my brother. Are you alright?

                    JESUS
        Shylamah my sister. Thank you for your
        concern.

JESUS looks at his feet. Then he looks at MARTA

                    JESUS (cont')
        And may I ask, what is your name?

                    MARTA
        I am MARTA. And you?

                    JESUS
        My mother and father gave me the name,
        EASHOA.

                    MARTA
        Oh I remember you-

                    JESUS
            (interupts)
        -Excuse me.
            (beat)
        Hey, MARTA I just need a little rest. Is

there an Inn where I can rent in this village?

                    MARTA
          No, your in the village of Bethany. But in
          in your condition, please follow me.

MARTA puts her arm around JESUS. He helps him walk to her small home on the south side of the village near lots of trees.

EXT. PORCH - EVENING

JESUS and MARTA stand on the porch of her home. MARTA opens the front door. JESUS limps into the small yet well-furnished warm cozy home. MARTA helps him to the couch and helps JESUS lies down.

MARTA walks out of the living room into her bedroom. She returns to living room with oil and bandages. She cleans and bandages his feet.

                                        FADE TO BLACK

INT. DINNING ROOM – MORNING

MARTA is cooking breakfast in the kitchen. Her long brown hair displays her true beauty. In the b.g., JESUS is sitting up on the couch drinking a warm cup of tea.

                    MARTA
          The food is ready. I prepared some bread,
          yogurt, vegetables and dried fruit.

MARTA walks over to JESUS. She places the food on a table in front of JESUS.

                    JESUS
          Thank you. MARTA. Normally, I work for
          my food before I eat. But my feet-
               (he laughs)

                    MARTA
               (interupts)
          -Your feet are in such bad shape, I can forgive
          you this time. You know it's going to take a few
          days before you can walk well again.

                    JESUS
          I know.

MARTA walks to the front door. She says, "I must leave for some other business. I shall see you this afternoon."

                    JESUS
          Peace, I'm not going anywhere over the next
          few days.

JESUS watches MARTA close the door. He takes a deep breath. He smiles. He begins eating. He is enjoying every bite.

                                                      FADE OUT:

INT. PALACE OF PONTIUS PILATE – DAY

FADE IN:

PONTIUS PILATE (60), white skin, clean shaven, curly blond hair, dressed in a Roman draped red Togo. He paces back and forth in his royal court. Standing next to a Marbled pillar is SEJANUS, olive tone skin, black beard, black hair wearing Roman Centurion garbs.

                    SEJANUS
          PILATE, my Judean Governorship, will not
          appease the Jews as much as you do.

                    PONTIUS PILATE
          SEJANUS, you are aware that your position
          contrasts with the revived imperial policy of
          TIBERIUS'S tenure? Rome does tolerate
          Paganism and Judaism.

                    SEJANUS
          PILATE, remember, I am the man who chose
          you to serve this position her in Jerusalem,
          not TIBERIUS!

                    PONTIUS PILATE
          You are coming very close to treason.

In walks the Jewish High Priest, CAIAPHAS, with six REPRESENTATIVES of the Jewish Sanhedrin (60 – 75), grey beards, wearing priestly garments. They are seated by two armed roman officers. In the b.g., SEJANUS and PILATE stand next to one another observing each Priest as they sit down. PILATE begins walking over to his throne. SEJANUS walks to a nearby cover.

                    PILATE
               (sitting down)
          CAIAPHAS, I glad you made it here safely.
          I understand you have an urgent matter
          to discuss with me.

                    CAIAPHAS (75)
          PONTIUS PILATE, thank you for your
          hospitality.
               (beat)
          We seem to have a problem.

PONTIUS PILATE
You people are always agitating Rome
with religious issues. Ohh, I agonize when
I think about being appointed to Jerusalem
as Rome's prefect in the province of Judaea.
I only have one-hundred Roman soldiers
Inside the walls of this city.
            (beat)
What is it now?

CAIAPHAS
We seem to have a Jebusite named JESUS
teaching against to religious order of the
Jews and Rome.

In the b.g., SEJANUS stands next to a roman officer. Both of them grimace.
PONTIUS PILATE slowly gets up. He steps down from his throne onto the polished
granite stone floor of the palace. Head down, hands folded behind his back, he paces
back and forth in front of the Sanhedrin Priest.

NARRATOR (V.O.)
As prefect of Rome, Pontius Pilate was
granted the power of a supreme judge,
which meant that he had the sole authority
to order a criminal's execution. His duties
as a prefect included such mundane tasks
as tax collection and managing construction
projects. But, perhaps his most crucial
responsibility was that of maintaining law
and order. Pontius Pilate attempted to do so
by any means necessary. What he couldn't
negotiate he is said to have accomplished
through brute force.

PONTIUS PILATE
Are you suggesting that I collaborate with
you against a poor Jebusite preacher?
            (beat)
Come now CAIAPHAS.

CAIAPHAS
Do you recall when the Great Herod beheaded
John for preaching God's judgement against-

PONTIUS PILATE
            (interupts)
-I rule Jerusalem now! Not Herod. He dead and gone.

PONTIUS PILATE walks over to the steps of his throne. He slowly sits down on his chair. He looks over at SEJANUS standing in the rear of the room by the marble pillar. Then he looks downward at the six Jewish Sanhedrin Representatives.

FADE OUT:

INT. HOME - LIVING ROOM - EVENING

JESUS is sitting on couch messaging his feet. MARTA open the front door. She walks into the house, stands at the front door looking at JESUS.

> MARTA
> Shylamah.

> JESUS
> Shylamah, how was your day?

> MARTA
> Very successful.

MARTA hangs her purse on a latch next to the door. She walks over to the kitchen and begins preparing a meal.

> MARTA
> There is a certain elder of our village
> who knows who you are JESUS. He
> wants to know if some of the people of
> our village can have an audience with
> you on the Mount of Olives?

> JESUS
> It will be my pleasure. I have visited the
> Mount to look at the city of Jerusalem.

CUT TO:

INT. SANHEDRIN COURT - NIGHT

CAIAPHAS and two SANHEDRIN JUDGES sit in the corner of the court hall.

> SANHEDRIN JUDGE 1
> Have we made a deal with ROME?

> CAIAPHAS
> And?

> SANHEDRIN JUDGE 1
> There is a reward out for his life. $1,500
> alive and $2,500 dead.

CAIAPHAS, looks dead serious as he nods his head with approval pulling on his whiskers.

CUT TO:

INT. HOME – MOUNT OF OLIVE – NIGHT

Eighteen MEN and WOMEN sit on mats. To the side blazes a lit fire. Several women serve tea, including MARTA. An OLD MAN, dark skin, thin grey beard, short gray curly hair walks JESUS into over the congregation of people to speak. The OLD MAN greets the gathering with the words, "Shylamah", now I turn the meeting over into the hands of EASHUA, son of MARYAM and YUSEF.

                         JESUS
          Thank you sir for allowing me to address
          the village elders. Because time is of the
          essence, I will get right into my talk. To
          begin, I competed my formal and spiritual
          education in Egypt. Although I am 33
          years old now, I was 14 years old at the
          time when the ancient priesthood of Egypt
          shared with me some of the mysteries of
          the ages-

                         MARTA
                    (interrupts)
          -What did they say, JESUS?

                         JESUS
                    (chuckes)
          Well let me start with the house of Israel
          —the Adamic Civilization.

                         WOMEN 1
          Who?

                         JESUS
          They were the race who initially invaded
          our lands arriving from the Aegean sea.
          At one time in our history, we called them
          Sea People.

The gathering of the people look astonished.

                         JESUS (cont')
          MARTA, the world is going to be ruled
          by this race for another 2000 years
          before God in the flesh is born to remove

them from power.
>   (beat)
I spoke these words to a chief priest several
weeks ago. Only I used a parable. Of course,
he was livid.

>   MAN 2
My Lord! This is an amazing truth! Aren't
you concerned for your life? Are in danger?

>   JESUS
The authorities can only catch me if I
allow then to catch me. I have a radio
in my head.
>   (smiling)
And no, I am not afraid. You shall
know the truth because the truth shall
set you free! We must continue to live
peaceful lives among ourselves, eat the
best food, do not eat swine flesh. We
must stay away from laziness and live
as if we preparing to enter into the
Kingdom of God. But most of all,
remember, as a man thinketh, so is he."

The people of the gathering begin to sing the praises of the Lord, repeating, "Alleluia and Alleluia!" The OLD MAN and MARTA walk up and stand on opposite sides where JESUS sits while the gathering of people walk up to touch his garments. One women says to the OLD MAN as she walks by, "I believe this man is the promised Messiah." After everyone leaves, JESUS is left alone for a moment crying. Looks up at the millions of stars thinking to himself, "I am 2,000 years to soon. Its little more left for me to teach in this Hellenized world order."

>   FADE OUT:

EXT. TEMPLE MOUNT – COURT YARD – DAY

SUPERIMPOSE: ONE YEAR LATER

The city of Jerusalem is packed with pilgrims from as far as South Europe to celebrate Passover. JESUS walks among the crowd. He enters Temple court yard of Jerusalem and stands in a corner to observe the activities. Within the Temple court yard are livestock, merchants and doves held in wicker-work cages. JESUS walks over to the money changer tables. He looks at certain priest exchanging standard Greek and Roman coins for Jewish and Tyrian coins with customers. He thinks to himself, "a den of thieves using the Temple of the people for commercial activities and give nothing back to the poor."

EXT. TEMPLE TOWER – DAY

Two JEWISH RABBI'S stand atop a tower platform. They both look glance outward into the streets of Jerusalem at the throngs of pilgrims. One of them turns his attention back into the Temple courtyard. He sees a black man waving this finger and pointing at a money changer.

> JEWISH RABBI 1
> Brother turn around and look at that Jebusite.

> JEWISH RABBI 2 (P.O.V.)
> (turns around)
> What is doing on over there? Is he arguing?

> JEWISH RABBI 1
> I don't know, but let go call the guard.

CUT TO:

EXT. MONEY CHANGER TABLE – DAY

JESUS is walking away from the money changer table. He slightly turns his head to the left and downward and stops for a moment. In his right ear, he hears a ringing sound, then fast moving footsteps and clanging armor. JESUS looks around for the nearest exit. He sees a door on the south side of the Temple and slips out.

CUT TO:

EXT. MONEY CHANGER TABLE – DAY

Two JEWISH RABBI'S sit on a bench next to three ROMAN OFFICERS standing next to the money changer table. A SOLDIER speaks with the MONEY CHANGER whom JESUS rebuked.

> ROMAN OFFICER 1
> Who was that trouble maker?

> MONEY CHANGER
> I not sure but I have a feeling he knows what
> we are doing here in the Temple.

> ROMAN OFFICER 1
> What do you mean?

JEWISH RABBI'S pay close attention looking straight into the mouth of the MONEY CHANGER.

> MONEY CHANGER
> He said, 'Make not my father's house a
> house a den of thieves and Merchandise.'
> He said 'religion should not be mixed
> with traffic, for traffic tends toward sin
> and that Phariseeism is its fruit...a wish
> to carry on profitable business, even with
> God.

JEWISH RABBI 2
Is that all?

ROMAN SOLDIER 1 stands on his toes looking out into the crowd.

MONEY CHANGER
Yes, one thing. He said, 'I find in the temple,
profaners, money-makers, sign-seekers,
oppose of reform, false and weak professors
of faith. I can trust none of you!'

ROMAN SOLDIER 2
RABBI, this sounds like the same man wanted
by Rome dead or alive.

RABBI 2
(devious look)
Yes I believe the reward is $1500 alive and
$2500 dead. Can you believe some people call
him the Christ.
(scoffs)
He's no Christ, He is a trouble maker!

FADE OUT:

INT. VILLIAGE OF BETHANY – LATE EVENING

Sheep rests outside the entrance leading into the village of Bethany. JESUS rides up on a donkey. He dismounts the donkey and pets the head of a little lamb before walking through the gates of Bethany.

CUT TO:

EXT. FRONT DOOR – LATE EVENING

FADE IN:

JESUS walks up to MARTA'S front door. He knocks. MARTA opens the door.

JESUS
Shylamah, MARTA

MARTA
Shylamah, JESUS—the giver of life.

JESUS smiles. MARTA invites JESUS into her home. He walks in and sees another women sitting in a chair.

MARTA
JESUS, this is my sister, TOMASSA.

                        JESUS
Shylamah

                        TOMASSA
                  (pointing at jesus)
I remember you!

                        JESUS
From where?

                        TOMASSA
                  (pleasant)
Oh, never mind. I must return to Jericho. Its
getting late. Anyhow, my husband awaits me.

EXT. PORCH – MARTA'S HOME - NIGHT

MARTA and TOMASSA stand on the front porch.

                        TOMASSA
               MARTA the next time I visit, you must
               share more of the teachings JESUS has
               shared with you. I hope you don't mind
               if I share it with my husband?

MARTA stretches both her arms outward and places both her hands on TOMASSA
shoulders. She looks at TOMASSA eye to eye shaking her head in the affirmative. Then
quietly says, "yes, yes; of course. Just tell him to spread the true word." TOMASSA
smiles and walks away.

MARTA walks back into the house. JESUS is sitting on the couch. He is rubbing his feet.

                        MARTA
               JESUS I have prepared a bath for you.
               Afterward I will oil you sore feet.

JESUS nods his head in the affirmative and smiles.

                                                      FADE TO BLACK:

EXT. STREETS OF BETHANY – MORNING

JESUS, wearing white robe and MARTA, wearing a black, red and green loose garment
and head scarf are walking down the street. He says, "Thank TOMASSA for making me
this beautiful white garment and her husband for giving me these fine leather sandals.
By the way, you will find a silver coin I found under your couch."

                        MARTA
                  (looks at sandals)
               Praise our lord.

In the f.g., JESUS sees a group of children (7-10) playing. He walks over to them. Some of the PARENTS of the children begin walking over toward JESUS and MARTA.

> JESUS
> (looks at parents)
> Let the children come to truth and do
> not refuse them, because the Kingdom
> of Heaven belongs to those who are like
> these.

> MARTA
> Please explain, sir.

> JESUS
> There hearts and minds are not yet filled
> with self-contention like the people of
> this world.

JESUS looks at the parents of the children.

> PARENT 1
> (cries out)
> Brother, look at our land, It has been
> usurped by foreigners. We are taxed till
> death.

> JESUS
> Brother I leave you with this: For, behold,
> the day cometh, that shall burn as an
> oven; and all the proud, yea, and all that
> do wickedly, shall be stubble: and the day
> that come shall burn them up, saith the
> LORD of hosts, that it shall leave them
> neither root nor branch. But unto you
> that fear my name shall the Sun of
> righteousness arise with healing in his
> wings; and you shall go forth, and grow
> up as calves of the stall. And you shall
> tread down the wicked; for they shall be
> ashes under the soles of your feet in the day
> that I shall do this, saith the LORD of hosts.
>
> Behold, I will send you Elijah the prophet
> before the coming of the great and dreadful
> day of the LORD: And he shall turn the heart
> of the fathers to the children, and the heart
> of the children to their fathers, lest I come
> and strike the earth with destruction.

The parents began looking at one another with mixed emotions. Some began whipping tears from their eyes. The children started running with joy, laughter and playing with one another. JESUS and MARTA continue walking. They stop at the village entrance. She looks at him. Storm clouds begin brewing in the sky overhead.

                    MARTA
          Who is Elijah?

                    JESUS
               (takes deep breath)
          Ohhh, he comes about 2,000 years after
          the Temple is ruined to the ground.

JESUS moves closer to MARTA. He gently hugs her and kisses her forehead.

                    JESUS (cont')
          In these few scrolls, I studies, I came to
          realized, I was born 2000 years to soon.

                    MARTA
               (tears in her eyes)
          What do you mean?

                    JESUS
               (smiling)
          The last Messenger of God, the Messiah
          and his people will be illiterate, lost in a
          strange land. They will need to be found
          the son of Man. He alone will raise them
          from a deep spiritual death, two fold the
          children of hell captured inside the house
          of Israel.

JESUS then grabs MARTA'S hands. He kisses both hands. Out nowhere, the VILLAGE ELDER, dress in all white robe, thin and bald head walks from behind the village wall with a colt.

                    VILLAGE ELDER
          JESUS you have walked long enough. Take
          this colt. Ride it down into Jerusalem on
          this day.

Rain begins to dribble out of the sky. JESUS mounts the colt. MARTA and the VILLAGE ELDER watch him ride down the long dirt road into the valley until he fades beyond their eyesight. MARTA looks at the VILLAGE ELDER, she says, "father what is going to happen to JESUS." He replies, "He is going to fulfil his portion of what he has learned about his divine mission and destiny."

                                        DISSOLVE:

EXT. STORE-FRONT – DARK CLOUDY DAY

SUPERIMPOSE: OLD JERUSALEM 36 AD

The day is dark, cloudy and raining. JESUS is standing under an awning in front of a store. A poorly dressed small diverse crowd slowly begin to gather around JESUS.

> NARRATOR (V.O.)
> It was raining that day. JESUS got himself
> a standing place under an awning of a JEW'S
> store and began teaching those who
> were stopping under the awning out of the
> rain. The old JEW who owned the store got
> angry with JESUS about teaching in front of
> his store and asked him to leave.

> JESUS
> Let me teach under your awning and
> people I am teaching will buy something
> from you.

> JEW
> But you are keeping those that might buy
> something from seeing my goods in the
> showcase.

> JESUS
> I don't care. If I leave here I will lose my
> people who are listening to me.

A crowd of twenty-five people have now gathered to watch the two men argue their points of view.

> JEW
> (pointing at jesus)
> I know who you are. You are the man
> called Jesus that the authorities have
> been looking for a long time.

> JESUS
> Yes I am the one. You can call them
> anytime you want to.

The crowd becomes restless. A black man in the crowd yells, "come on let the brother teach!" Thunder and lightning is heard and frightens some people in the crowd. JESUS dismisses the congregation. The JEWISH store owner (65), pale white skin retreats back into his store. He confronts his CLERK (14), dark olive skin boy, curly hair, green eyes.

JEW

Go right away to let the authorities know
the trouble maker, Christ, is at my door.

CLERK

Right away sir.

The CLERK grabs a hooded overcoat and runs out of the front door. JESUS watches the boy running down the street.

SERIES OF SHOTS

(1) CLERK running down the street

(2) CLERKS hands moving frantically as he stands before two ROMAN OFFICERS

(3) One Africanized Roman soldier and one white Roman soldier run down the street, their knives sheaths hand swing back and forth

(4) JESUS stands their under the awning looking fearless and resolute. He hears in right ear running footsteps and clanging armor, yet he does not run

(5) MARTA siting in her house, holding her stomach with one hand and face with the other hand. She is crying.

NARRATOR (V.O.)

The CLERK runs around the corner to get
the authorities. He sees two ROMAN OFFICERS
to inform them that JESUS was teaching right
in front of his store and they must come over
right away to catch him. Two OFFICERS ran to
the scene knowing there was a reward out for
JESUS.

The reward was twenty-five hundred in gold
(not 30 pieces of silver) if he was brought in
dead, and fifteen hundred dollars if he were
brought in alive. So these TWO OFFICERS
raced down to the old Jew's store where said
JESUS was. Each of the officers wanted the
reward. JESUS knew that they were coming
and made no effort to leave because he
intended for them to kill him. He realized he
was 2,000 years to soon before the Adamic
Civilization would be remove from power.

END SERIES OF SHOTS

EXT. STOREFRONT – RAINING - DAY

SLOW MOTION:

The two ROMAN OFFICERS (six feet tall) rushed up to JESUS, 5'6', 120 lbs. Each man trying to be the first to lay hands on him. When both OFFICERS came near to JESUS, they touched him practically at the same time.

END SLOW MOTION

                    ROMAN OFFICER 1
          He is mine!

                    ROMAN OFFER 2
          No, he's mine! I got here first!

Both soldiers huffing and puffing for a breath of fresh air.

                    ROMAN OFFICER 1
          No I was here first!

JESUS seeing them arguing and disputing about him, said to them. "Will you let me help you settle this argument. I will tell you who was the first man to put his hands on me?" The soldier both agreed by nodding their heads.

                    JESUS
          The man on the right side touched me
          one-tenth of a second before the one on
          the left.

                    NARRATOR (V.O.)
          So the one on the left lost the reward.
          The one on the right who won took JESUS
          by the walking him toward the jail.

EXT. STREET CORNER – DAY- LIGHTLY RAINING

ROMAN OFFICER and JESUS reached a street corner down the street from the jail. The ROMAN OFFICER is holding JESUS by the wrist. In the f.g., the jail can be seen. The ROMAN OFFICER suddenly stops. He walks JESUS into a side alley.

                    ROMAN OFFICER
          Listen I will only get fifteen hundred
          dollars in gold for carrying you in alive,
          but if I carry you to them they are going to
          kill you anyway, so why not let me kill you
          and make the twenty-five hundred dollars
          as I am a poor man and have a wife and
          family to care for?"

JESUS stares at the passersby's on the main street adjacent to the alleyway. They are scurrying about to get out of the rain. The ROMAN OFFICER grabs JESUS and begins walking further down the alleyway.

> NARRATOR (V.O.)
> JESUS knew he would be killed but did
> not care. So JESUS agreed with the officer
> that he would let him kill him so he could
> get the bigger reward. So he walked down
> the street where a Jew's store was vacant
> with boards and nailed over the front to
> secure the safety of the store.

EXT. ABANDON STORE FRONT – CLOUDY DARK DAY

BOTH JESUS and the ROMAN OFFICIER stand in front of a boarded up building.

> ROMAN OFFICER
> Right here is all right! Now put your back
> against the wall and hold your hands up.

JESUS had no fear in his eyes. He put his hands up and straightened himself and put his arms straight across the storefront flat against the boards.

IN SLOW MOTION

MONTAGE – VARIOUS

- ROMAN OFFICERS raises knife above his head, hand clutches knife tightly
- JESUS facial expression is fearless. He stands against a board building with both arms stretched out

- Knife plunges in JESUS chest. The old wooden board vibrates below JESUS'S left arm pit.

- ROMAN OFFICER jumps back. His facial expression is full of fear with very little blood splash

- JESUS'S head slightly falls back toward the right side, eyes closed. He dies instantly. His body is pinned upright to wooden board with knife in his heart; both arms stretched out wide.

END MONTAGE- END SLOW MOTION

EXT. JAIL CENTER FOOTSTEPS – DARK CLOUDY DAY

ROMAN OFFICER drops the board with JESUS'S body on the footsteps of the jail facing upward. His head is angled downward at the step bottom and his feet upward at the step top. The ROMAN OFFICER views the body. He sees very little blood before walking inside the jail. PASSERBY'S watch in horror seeing a lifeless black body sitting upside down on the footsteps of the jail center. Two BLACK WOMEN stop. One of them looks closer at the body.

                    BLACK WOMEN 1
          There goes another brother dead at the
          hands of the authorities.

                    BLACK WOMEN 2
          Hey this looks like E-SHO.

                    BLACK WOMEN 1
          Who?

                    BLACK WOMEN 2
          We lived on the same street years ago. Hurry,
          let's get out of here! I must let his people know!

The TWO WOMEN quickly walk away across the street. Both look over their shoulders. Then they turn the corner.

                                        CUT TO:

INT. TEA SHOP – RAINING- EVENING

MARYAM standing around a group of friends. INRAM sits a table drinking tea. Suddenly a light flashes before MARYAM'S eyes, she faints. Before she hits the ground, INRAM catches her before she hits the floor. He lays her down gently.

                    INRAM
               (panick)
          MARYAM, MARYAM are you okay?
               (beat)
          Someone please bring her some water,
          Hurry, hurry!

MARYAM head slowly moves side to side. She is moaning in sorrow, "no, no, no, my E-SHO, my E-SHO."

                    INRAM
          Has something happen to my grandson!

                                        CUT TO:

INT. JAIL CENTER – NIGHT

ROMAN OFFICER speaks with his SUPERIOR at a desk.

                    SUPERIOR
          You did a good job. That, that Egyptian

necromancer has aggravated Roman
provinces for 22 years. We could never
caught him until now.

In the b.g., the body of JESUS lies flat on the cold brick floor covered in a brown
shroud. Both his arms hang out the extremes of the blanket.

                    ROMAN OFFICER
               (shivering)
          Who is he?

                    SUPERIOR
               (looks over at dead body)
          We found out that he is the son of JOSEPH.
          His mothers name is MARY. Joseph still
          lives in Jerusalem. We do not have any
          whereabouts where his mother resides.

                    ROMAN OFFICER
               (shivering)
          All I'm concerned with is my 2,500 dollar reward.

Other officers walk over and pat him on the back, all repeating, "good job, good job.
The sound of thunder rumbles above the sky.

                                        CUT TO:

INT. PALACE – HOT POOL – NIGHT

Hot steaming pool surrounded by marble floors, gold laced pillars. Male and female
servants scantily dressed, serve grapes and wine to the guest. PONTIUS PILATE sits in
the corner of the pool. A male servant brings him a cup of wine.

A JEWISH RABBI enters the hot pool deck and quickly walks over toward PONTIUS
PILATE. He leans down close to his ear.

                    JEWISH RABBI
               (whispers)
          The child whose father acted like a ghost
          is no more.

                    PONTIUS PILATE
               (sips wine)
          Well, you have your wish. An innocent man
          is dead.
               (sips wine)
          Now leave me or join my party.

                                        CUT TO:

INT. CONSTRUCTION SITE – JERICO – MORNING

A YOUNG MAN riding a donkey through a construction site. He rides by a nice mud brick home and sees several construction WORKERS polishing some bricks in the front of a house. He gets off the donkey and walks over to the group of men.

                    YOUNG MAN
          Excuse me brother, can anyone point out
          YUSEF? I have an urgent message for him.

                    WORKER1
          He is our father. You can find him around
          the back of the house.

                    YOUNG MAN
          Thank you.

The YOUNG MAN walks to the back of the house. YUSEF sees the YOUNG MAN walking toward him.

                    YUSEF
               (smiling)
          How can I help?

                    YOUNG MAN
          Are you the man they can YUSEF?

                    YUSEF
          Yes my brother. How may I help you?

                    YOUNG MAN
          It grieves me to inform you that JESUS is
          dead.

YUSEF closes his eyes, slowly raises his head back to the sky. He takes a deep breath clinching his fist. Then he walks over to his colt, mounts the colt and quickly rides down a dirt trial.

                                        FADE OUT:

INT. ROMAN JAIL CENTER – NIGHT

YUSEF stands over the body of JESUS. Behind him are three other Jebusites. YUSEF notices how JESUS is stretched out in the form of a cross lying on three wooden slabs. He thinks to himself, "I wonder why there is very blood splatter." Then he kneels down and kisses JESUS on his forehead.

                                        CUT TO:

INT. HOUSE OF AMORAH – MORNING

FADE IN:

SUPERIMPOSE: OLD JERUSALEM

A smooth wooden table sits in the center of a sterile room. The body of JESUS lie on the table. Arms to the side, body covered in a white garment. Only his face can be seen. In the f.g. two BLACK MEN (40), bald heads, goat tees, no mustache, wearing loose fitting slacks with no shirts stand next to YUSEF.

> BLACK MAN 1
> Welcome to the house of Amorah.

> YUSEF
> I understand you are the best embalmers
> in Jerusalem.

> BLACK MAN 1
> Yes my brother. We were both trained in
> Egypt.

> YUSEF
> (stutters)
> Why, why wasn't there more blood spillage
> on the sons body?

> BLACK MAN 2
> It appears your son was unafraid upon impact
> when he was struck in the heart by the knife
> The lack of fear would have frozen the blood
> flow immediately rather than splatter.

> BLACK MAN 2
> Brother YUSEF, down in Egypt, we would say
> your son had the heart of lion, a warrior.

> YUSEF
> (saddened)
> Praise God. I want his body to last as long as
> the earth, but I am not able to pay for such
> embalmment. So I am willing to pay 10,000
> dollars to embalm the body of my son to last
> 10,000 years.

YUSEF looks over at JESUS'S body lying on the table.

> YUSEF (cont')
> Can you make this happen?

BLACK MAN 2
Yes we can. The total process will take around
70 days to complete.

FADE OUT:

INT. HOUSE OF AMORAH - BASMENT- NIGHT

JESUS'S body lies inside a tub-like table several feet from the ground. Two BLACK MEN are pouring water over the body, cleaning the body.

BLACK MAN 1
This is a righteous man we are embalming.

BLACK MAN 2
Yes, he is one of our brothers. Let's do are best to preserve him very well. Later we will encapsulate his body inside a glass tube that shall arrive from Egypt soon.

MONTAGE - VARIOUS

- Water pouring down the face of JESUS

- Water pouring over chest of JESUS

- The feet of JESUS being wrapped in white cloth

- JESUS entire body wrapped in white cloth except his face

END MONTAGE

INT. HOUSE OF AMORAH - SOUTH END OF UPPER ROOM - DAY

SUPERIMPOSE: 70 DAYS LATER

Through a window, rays of light beam upon the glass tube containing JESUS. He appearance looked the same as if he were alive.

Standing around the glass tube are YUSEF, his six children, MARYAM, several of her relatives, INRAM, TOMASSA and MARTA (pregnant with child). Everyone is dressed in white. No one is crying, everyone looks at the body of JESUS with astonishment.

NARRATOR (V.O.)
The Egyptian embalmers had filled the glass tube with a certain chemical (known only to Egyptian embalmers) that will keep one's body looking the same as when it died. So this is how the preserved JESUS.

FADE TO BLACK:

INT. HOUSE OF AMORAH – BASEMENT – NOON

Two EYGPTIAN EMBALMERS lead YUSEF, his six children, MARYAM, several of her relatives, INRAM, TOMASSA and MARTA down into a well-lit basement lined with oil lamps. When they reach the glass tube containing the body of JESUS in the ground surrounded by a wooden floor, they see the glass tube sparkling.

CAMERA CLOSE UP:

FRESH AND CLEAN FACE OF JESUS WRAPPED IN WHITE EGYPTIAN CLOTHE.

THE END

www.ingramcontent.com/pod-product-compliance
Lightning Source LLC
Chambersburg PA
CBHW062359220526
45472CB00008B/1869